Public Purposes in Broadcasting: Funding the BBC

Public Purposes in Broadcasting: Funding the BBC

UNIVERSITY
OF LUTON

press

British Library Cataloguing in Publication Data
A catalogue record for this book is available from the British Library

ISBN: 1 86020 561 5

Published by
University of Luton Press
University of Luton
75 Castle Street
Luton
Bedfordshire LU1 3AJ
United Kingdom

Tel: +44 (0)1582 743297; Fax: +44 (0)1582 743298
e-mail: ulp@luton.ac.uk

Cover Design by Gary Gravatt
Typeset in Palatino and Helvetica
Printed in Great Britain by Whitstable Litho, Whitstable, Kent

Contents

Foreword

Broadcasting is a British success story. Audiences have been well served by strong networks as well as fast growing new services. Entrepreneurs are turning the UK into a digital test-bed, with near simultaneous launches of digital channels via both satellite and cable systems and terrestrial transmitters. Use of the Internet is booming and new technology can offer broadcast, on demand and one-to-one communications combined, through either televisions or personal computers.

Britain's broadcasting and telecommunication industries are world class. As their technologies converge, they have the potential to drive real economic growth via a vibrant, combined service sector. But can we encourage that dynamic without losing the cultural and social benefits associated with what has been a strongly regulated broadcasting industry?

Audiences are now experiencing the shift from a shared experience of four or five free-to-air television networks to a choice of hundreds of subscription or pay-per-view offerings; from half a dozen radio services to scores; from *News at Ten* to the ability to access personalised news headlines online at any time. It is a revolutionary shift.

There are real fears that more will mean worse, that competition will fragment audiences and investment across multiple outlets, leading to tabloid values and to a nation divided between those who embrace the new services and those who either cannot afford or do not wish to do so.

The challenge for public policy is to deliver the best of both worlds; to drive growth and to sustain quality. Deregulation of the commercial sector has, therefore, been balanced with a greater focus on the role and responsibility of public service broadcasting, in the shape of the BBC. The last Government sought to define requirements for public service in a new ten-year Charter and Agreement. It even increased the level of the licence fee – for the first time in fifteen years – to pay for them.

The new Labour Government has now established its own review of the BBC, re-opening the debate about public purpose and funding. These essays are commissioned as a contribution to that debate. They start, as does the Review, from the premise that society has particular expectations of broadcasting which the new and expanding commercial market cannot

1

guarantee to meet. Each essay then explores aspects of the funding and delivery of those public expectations and purpose.

The views expressed are those of the authors and not necessarily of the BBC. But the BBC's own thinking has been much influenced by the themes developed here.

In summary, these essays suggest an even greater need for investment in standard setting programmes as the market fragments. They reaffirm the importance of services that inform, educate and entertain in ways the market alone will not. And they propose new social and educational purposes for the BBC in a digital world, based on inclusiveness and a mission to bridge the gap between the information rich and the information poor. They remind us that particular forms of funding produce programmes and services with particular characteristics; that advertising tends to require broadcasters to concentrate on the tried and popular – to narrow range – whilst subscription fails to maximise value for all. The case for public service broadcasting remains that it not only provides funding for the production of programmes – demonstrably valued by viewers and listeners – that would not otherwise be made, but that it then popularises and extends the reach of such programmes.

These essays are a major contribution to debate about what audiences should expect of the BBC beyond 2000. They chime with purposes that the BBC has recently reaffirmed:

- to create programmes and services of real cultural value, supporting the rich diversity of the UK's heritage and identity and to ensure, through news and factual programming, that all sides join in the debate on issues of national, regional or local significance;
- to provide something of particular value to all, helping people broaden their horizons through learning and by enriching their skills;
- to expose audiences to new insights and ideas, offering stimulus and delight and providing opportunities for talent in every field.

And they inform new purposes:

- to ensure no-one is excluded from access to new kinds of service made possible by new technology;
- to use the BBC's ability to reach into every home to engage audiences in new experiences and to act as a trusted guide in a world of abundance.

In a world of vigorous competition, public purposes for broadcasting can still, then, deliver national benefits:

- supporting citizenship and democracy, guaranteeing access to the full range of information necessary for individuals to make informed choices, whether as voters, consumers or simply as members of society;

- bringing benefit to Britain; with programmes and services that are successful around the world, a showcase for British talent and the gold standard for news and information.

Patricia Hodgson[1]

---

1   Patricia Hodgson is the BBC's Director of Policy & Planning and commissioned these essays as a contribution to the BBC's forward thinking. Particular thanks are also due to Dominic Morris and Simon Milner.

Executive Summary

1 Broadcasting Policy in the Multimedia Age

Andrew Graham

Andrew Graham argues that, even in the new world of global communications, subscription television and the Internet, there is a real need to support public purposes in broadcasting. The nature of 'information goods' makes *market failure* highly likely and public policy intervention necessary. In addition, new technology creates strong pressures towards an industry which is competitive, but where audiences are fragmented while ownership is concentrated. These two themes mean the market on its own cannot produce the full benefits of the new technology for society as a whole.

1.1 Market failures occur in broadcasting because information is difficult to sell normally (consumers do not know what they are buying until they have the information, but once they have the information they no longer need to buy it). In addition, broadcasting can have adverse effects that are 'external' to the market (eg amplifying violence in society), which it is not possible to correct through a pricing mechanism. Finally, quality broadcasting has the characteristics of a 'merit' good; just as with education and training or health checks, consumers, if left to themselves tend to buy less than is in their own long term interests. Without positive pressure in the system, there is a real danger that broadcasting, instead of expanding our horizons, will 'dumb us down'.

— *Citizenship and community:* As citizens we all have rights to core information about our own society, and many rely on broadcasting to deliver that information. This is not something the market would provide. As members of a community we have views about society that cannot be captured just in our buying and selling. Our collective and individual capacities for imagination and achievement are affected by 'the company we keep'. Broadcasting is today part of this company. The

5

communications system we, as a society, choose and the quality of the content that it carries will therefore be an important influence on the social values and concerns of the communities of the twenty first century.

— *Democracy:* It is a basic principle of a democratic society that votes should not be bought and sold. This alone is sufficient justification for broadcasting not being entirely commercial. The creation and sustenance of 'common knowledge' (what everyone knows that everyone knows) is a vital element in the functioning of democracy. In order to be *agreed,* solutions have to be based on a common understanding of the situation. The absence of common knowledge is a factor behind many of the co-ordination problems in democratic societies. Such 'common knowledge' is not well guarded by commercial markets.

— *Industrial Policy:* By a clever mix of the public and the private, the UK has managed to generate for itself a 'comparative advantage' in broadcasting. The UK's success has been led by the BBC and is the result of extensive investment in talent over many years.

1.2 The impact of changing technology on markets suggests a further danger that the new technology will replace public monopolies with private monopolies. Monopolies are *always* a matter for concern, but in a democratic society private monopolies in the media must be a matter for *special* concern:

— The new technology creates strong pressures towards a broadcasting industry where *audiences are fragmented and yet ownership is concentrated.* This is because high quality multimedia content is expensive to produce, but relatively cheap to edit or to change and trivially cheap to reproduce. It therefore has high fixed costs and low marginal costs – the natural creators of monopolies.

— High quality material can still be produced and yet cost very little *per unit* provided that it reaches a large number of people (exploiting economies of scale) and/or provided that it is used in a wide variety of different formats (exploiting economies of scope), but the exploitation of these economies of scale and scope imply concentration of ownership.

— Thus, while one source of monopoly, spectrum scarcity, has gone, it has been replaced with another – the natural monopoly of economies of scale and scope on the one hand plus the natural scarcity of talent on the other.

— In addition, bottlenecks in gateways mean that *particular* consumers may well become reliant on a *single* supplier. If so, it will be like being able to shop at Tesco, but *only at Tesco.*

1.3 The implication of these two themes is that the market *on its own* cannot produce the full benefits of the new technology for society as a whole. Equally the deficiencies in the market cannot be filled just by negative regulation. Current and future technical changes with broadcasting and the Internet operating globally, and with more intense commercial pressures makes regulation *less* effective. Rules are not appropriate for judging quality (and quality, by definition, cannot be measured - if it could, it would be quantity).

1.4 What public policy therefore requires is a *positive* force that would:

— act as a counterweight to the private concentration of ownership;

— deliver *national coverage* so as to counteract fragmentation of audiences;

— provide a 'centre of excellence' which both makes and broadcasts programmes;

— be large enough to influence the market and so act as the guarantor of quality;

— and widen choice both now and in the future by complementing the market through pursuit of public service purposes.

1.5 The best way to provide this positive pressure is via public service broadcasting (not as a substitute to the commercial sector but as a complement to it). While a public service broadcaster, such as the BBC, has no *right* to exist, there are *purposes for its existence*. Contrary to the conventional wisdom, the new technology *increases, rather than decreases, the need* for such a broadcaster.

1.6 The form of funding for such a broadcaster is crucial. Direct funding from Government is not appropriate because:

— the institution must be seen to be, and must believe itself to be, at arm's length from Government;

— the institution must be able to take a medium-term approach to its future plans which direct annual funding would not permit;

— and secure, long-term funding enables the institution to resist the temptation to boost its income through commercial sources, thus confusing its purpose.

1.7 Advertising and sponsorship, even if introduced only at the margin initially, would not be suitable forms of finance for the BBC. It would almost certainly be forced to proceed further down such routes each year until eventually it becomes indistinguishable from a commercial broadcaster. The licence fee comes closest to the ideal form of funding for public service broadcasting which should:

— create a direct link for consumers between the benefits they receive and the outlays made;

— involve the same charge for everyone;

— involve some income buoyancy so the charge grows faster than nominal GDP;

7

- be subject to minimum interference from the Government of the day;
- and be relatively easy to collect, enforce and administer.

2 The Implications of Funding for Broadcasting Output
Christian Koboldt, Sarah Hogg and Bill Robinson

The authors focus on the economics of broadcasting, examining the dynamics of different forms of funding and their impact on programming decisions. Three broad revenue sources are analysed: advertising, pay TV (pay-per–view and subscription), and the licence fee. Each of them creates incentives to make different types of programme and offer different types of service. The authors model these incentives to suggest the range of programming which is guaranteed by licence fee funding and not by other systems - in particular, programmes such as serious drama which are popular but do not necessarily maximise audience numbers.

2.1 Television programmes are not like bread. If one person eats a loaf of bread, it is not available for someone else to eat, but one person watching a television programme still leaves that programme available for others to watch. While it therefore makes sense to put a price on bread that *excludes* those who do not value bread at its cost of production and ensures bread is available for those who do, television programmes are different. Once they are on the air it costs nothing if one extra viewer tunes in.

2.2 This is the long-standing justification for using licence fees or advertising revenues to pay for the production of programmes which are then broadcast free of charge. The case for public service broadcasting is that the total enjoyment of all the viewers watching all the programmes made by the BBC is much greater than the cost of making them. In this sense the nation makes a 'profit' on the licence fee.

2.3 The chief problem with charging via subscription is that as soon as a charge is being made, some viewers will decide not to watch the programme or channel. The enjoyment they might have had is lost. This is the welfare cost of moving towards pay television. The benefit of introducing prices is that it can allow viewers to indicate which programmes they prefer *and how much they value them.* Until now broadcasting has largely been about *numbers* of viewers. Yet more value may be created by making a programme that is hugely enjoyed by a small number of people than by a programme watched – but not much enjoyed – by millions.

2.4 Public service broadcasters have always made such programmes, but find it difficult to decide which minorities to serve. The new technology allows the price mechanism to be used to allocate resources to the programmes which create most value. So minority sports such as club rugby are now available on subscription. But there are certain kinds of expensively produced programme which are only made by public service broadcasters.

2.5 This is fundamentally because different funding mechanisms induce different kinds of behaviour. Public service broadcasters are mandated to consider the *total value of the programme* to all who watch it. The commercial broadcaster is only interested in *that part of the value that can be captured*, whether via advertising revenue or via subscriptions. The total value of a programme is the revenue raised by charging each individual viewer the maximum that he or she would pay to watch it.

2.6 Only an all-powerful and omniscient broadcaster who did an individual deal with each viewer could capture this value. Ordinary pay TV broadcasters simply set a price. They fail to capture revenue from those who would have cheerfully paid a higher price. And they get no revenue from those who decide not to buy.

2.7 A criticism often levelled at advertising funding is that the capturable value only depends on the number of viewers. It does not matter how much the viewers enjoy the programme, only that they do not switch off. So advertising funding encourages broadcasters to spend only the minimum required to keep the largest possible audience watching.

2.8 Subscription or pay-per-view television deals with this problem to some extent, but not entirely:

— If the programme is of the kind for which there are passionately interested small audiences, it is easy to capture most of the value. The fanatics willingly pay the cost of producing the programme. The vast majority of those excluded by the price were not interested in watching it anyway.

— If the programme is of the kind where there are large audiences, of which a minority value the programme very highly (eg the Cup Final), it is difficult to capture the full value. If the price is set high, to capture its value to the football fans, millions may be excluded. If the price is set low to ensure that these millions do view the programme, most of the revenue that could have been extracted from the fans is lost.

2.9 The case for public service broadcasting funded by a licence fee is that it enables the production of programmes – valued by viewers – that would not otherwise be made. The case has always been strong when the only alternative is advertising revenues. It remains strong even when full account is taken of the increasing number of channels and potential for more pay-TV. There are programmes whose full value to the viewers cannot be captured by the new charging mechanisms currently on offer. There is still therefore a risk that in the absence of a licence fee funded broadcaster such programmes would simply not be made.

2.10 Even a partial dependence on commercial sources of income tends to introduce the same pressures and incentives faced by fully commercial broadcasters. If, for example, the BBC were mainly licence fee funded, but partly dependent on advertising revenue, it would for this part of its income be subject to the same incentive to maximise revenues (i.e., the same pressure to compete for them) as a broadcaster funded entirely by advertising.

3 The BBC: Balancing Public and Commercial Purposes
David Currie and Martin Siner

The authors consider the issues raised by the commercial activities of the BBC. They point out that the BBC owns numerous assets created in the pursuit of its public service role which have a secondary value that can be realised in the broader commercial marketplace through sales, licensing and joint ventures, and then used to support public service broadcasting. If the BBC were to neglect these commercial opportunities, it would be failing to make the best use of licence fee funds and jeopardising its pre-eminent position in the broadcasting industry (as other broadcasters experience significant revenue growth from the launch of digital channels). The case for these activities is a 'no-brainer'.

3.1 The BBC has engaged in commercial activities from its beginning since the original publication and sale of the *Radio Times* and these activities represent a key support to the BBC's public purposes. The development of multi-channel television and the spread of digital broadcasting makes the BBC's commercial activities even more important, to boost its income to cope with rising rights costs, in the context of relatively flat licence fee income and to exploit the opportunities offered by new technology.

3.2 This raises a number of important second-level issues about the co-existence of public service and commercial activities in the BBC:

— First, what should determine whether activities are to be publicly or commercially funded? Both economic and public service criteria should be used. Activities involving high fixed costs and zero or low marginal costs should be licence-fee funded, provided they also fulfil public service roles. So for example, BBC One and BBC Two are public service activities both because of their economic characteristics (high fixed costs and zero - or low - marginal costs) and their public service roles (through helping shape a wider sense of community by educating, entertaining and informing). The appropriate funding of new delivery mechanisms as they evolve needs to be considered in the light of these criteria.

— The integrity of core public service BBC brand needs to be protected in developing commercial activities. This has a number of implications. Commercial activities should stem from BBC programming - the BBC should not be selling products or services (eg holidays or insurance) unrelated to its core activities. The BBC should also communicate actively to the public the rationale and criteria for its commercial services, since confusion will otherwise obfuscate the case for the licence fee.

— A uniquely complex set of constraints require the BBC to account for public funding (both licence fee and grant-in-aid) while meeting the objectives laid out in its Charter and satisfying general competition law. These constraints are appropriate. However, excessive rigidity in the monitoring of public service funds (especially in the division between licence fee and grant-in-aid) may reduce the scope for deriving desirable synergies and efficiencies to the detriment of Government and licence fee payers' interests.

— It is appropriate that the BBC's commercial and public service activities are structurally separated within the BBC because the skills required for success differs between them. Complete separation - through the sale of the BBC's commercial operations - would, however, be dangerous since the synergies between the public and commercial arms would then be lost. A strategic partnership should be developed between the two parts to recognise the key inter-dependence between them and to realise shared interests and objectives.

— There needs to be effective oversight of the commercial activities by the senior BBC management and the Governors, to ensure that the commercial activities do not compromise the BBC brand and are synergistic with the overall objectives of the BBC. To be effective, this oversight needs to be light-handed, operate within clearly defined principles and avoid micro-management.

4 Competition and Public Purpose: the European Approach
Graham Mather

Graham Mather examines the European context for the UK debate about the BBC's public purposes and its funding, exploring the contradictions between Europe's systems of support for public service broadcasting and European competition law. In some EU countries state supported public service remits and funding systems conflict with the competition requirements in the Treaty of Rome. The UK model for the BBC, with complete separation between its public service and commercial operations, suggests a way through the conflict.

4.1 Competition law cannot be applied across the board to broadcasting issues because of different national and regional cultural and public policy preferences, in particular the desire for broadcasting arrangements which capture the history, culture, preferences and ethos of different societies.

4.2 Complaints which have been hanging fire since 1991 make it essential for the European Commission to provide a methodology to allow problems of state aid and distortion of competition to be resolved.

4.3 Three potential solutions have been suggested:

— A tender system for public broadcasting would be inflexible and at odds with the dynamics of the development of modern innovative public service broadcasting.

— A dual model in which public service broadcasters could run public service and commercial roles within the same structure, would create impossible boundary problems and also lead to bureaucrats making programme decisions.

— A split financing system in which state support can only go to public service broadcasters whilst advertising, sponsorship or commercial income can go only to a commercial operator (which may be a commercial subsidiary of a public service broadcaster with adequate regulatory checks) would solve these problems, maximise transparency, and increase competition.

4.4 In the UK, the BBC has already moved in this direction with the support of Government. The BBC's commercial subsidiary BBC Worldwide and a robust fair trading system to police the boundary of public service and commercial broadcasting is an essential underpinning to the BBC's status in this context as a model European public service broadcaster.

5 Broadcasting and Public Purposes in the New Millennium
Julian Le Grand and Bill New

The authors examine the public purpose of broadcasting and the BBC in the context of new thinking about society's values. The BBC exists to respond to the needs and wants of its funders - the licence fee payers. But in addition the terms 'public service' and 'audience need', used *in addition to* audience wants, imply a social purpose. What these might be are explored under the headings of community, opportunity, responsibility and accountability.

5.1 It is clear the BBC is not a mouthpiece of Government or a crude instrument of social engineering - indeed its source of funding is designed to guarantee its independence from such pressures. Rather it has the responsibility to reflect and respond to society's own concerns. Four aspects of what may be described as "the value base" of society with particular salience at the turn of this century are Community,

Opportunity, Responsibility and Accountability. How could and should broadcasting in general and the BBC in particular support these values?

— *Community:* broadcasting has the unique ability to allow a large number of people to share in consumption of a single product at the same time. In so doing, it can promote a more integrated national community; combat fragmentation and polarisation through shared educational opportunities; illustrate how a successful society depends on mutual understanding and respect; and provide a foothold in society for those who feel marginalised or excluded.

— *Opportunity:* broadcasting can facilitate the acquisition of skills, from basic literacy and numeracy to the advanced teachings of the Open University; it can widen the knowledge base of individuals in a more general way and provide insights into 'the enormous variety of life's opportunities...' opening new avenues of enjoyment and fulfilment previously judged to be 'not for us'.

— *Responsibility:* the role of broadcasting in promoting personal responsibility is limited by concerns about individual freedom and independence of any political agendas, but the use of the media, for example, to combat crime or to increase awareness of health issues has been broadly accepted.

— *Accountability:* a vigorous media is essential to holding government, institutions and individuals to account; broadcasting - uniquely - allows viewers and listeners to judge for themselves what a politician or other professional has to say; it provides access and a range of information essential to the healthy functioning of democracy.

5.2 In all these categories, the commercial broadcasting market has much to offer, but may not lead to optimum outcomes. The BBC, with its particular combination of funding and responsibility can and does:

— provide greater range and depth of coverage of national events, such as elections, than would be justified in terms of ratings;

— focus on services for a wider range of groups, including low income groups, than would be of interest to advertisers or shareholders;

— offer opportunities for new or demanding types of programming, including educational programming, without first needing to establish 'demand';

— set standards for responsible programming when the pure pressure to achieve ratings is eroding standards;

— investigate wrong-doing without concern about potential loss of commercial revenues from the firm or sector concerned, and;

— respond to 'needs' not 'wants', based on a collective judgement about how markets can fail.

5.3 However, public purpose depends on values or principles which are subjective and open to interpretation; there is a constant danger of striking an inappropriate balance or imposing values through the power of broadcasting, so particular accountability arrangements are needed to ensure the BBC's editorial policies accord with society's prevailing values. The licence fee mechanism has a particular role to play as a means of encouraging the individual viewer to act with vigilance in holding the BBC to account in pursuing its public purposes, in addition to the role of an independent Board, and governance by a Royal Charter. Public debate and negotiation around the terms of the BBC's Charter and Agreement is another means of approaching this issue.

5.4 But the biggest threat facing the BBC is the explosion of competition in the digital world, which could erode its ability to attract large audiences for public purpose programming. The BBC will need to work harder to retain a critical mass of viewers and - paradoxically - become more expert at competing for relevance and ratings if it is to deliver its public service objectives.

6 Broadcasting and the Socially Excluded
Ian Corfield

Ian Corfield addresses the question 'how does and should broadcasting, and particularly the BBC, serve the socially excluded?'. He examines the salient features of social exclusion in the UK today, its causes and how it might develop over the next decade. The actual and potential role of broadcasting in serving the social excluded is analysed with a specific focus on how the BBC might serve such groups better. Finally, the author examines the implications of the new media revolution for the social excluded. He sets rigorous challenges for the BBC to help ensure that the socially excluded do not become even more disconnected from society as a result of this revolution.

6.1 Poverty and social exclusion are often wrongly seen as synonymous by politicians and the Press. They are clearly closely related since many socially excluded people are evidently in poverty. But social exclusion is a combination of both material and non-material inequalities and thus many people in relative poverty may not be socially excluded.

6.2 There are four main groups with high concentrations of socially excluded people: poor pensioners; single parents; unemployed men, particularly young unemployed men; and some ethnic minorities. On current trends, three particular problems associated with social exclusion are likely to be reinforced. Economic divisions between those in secure work, those in insecure work and those not in work will become entrenched. There will be an ever increasing division between the information haves and the information have-nots. Finally there will be increasing problems associated with an ageing society.

6.3 Broadcasting serves the socially excluded principally through the provision of free-to-air broadcasting. This has always been one way in which everyone is connected to the world around them. The BBC is not alone in providing this service.

6.4 The main commercial broadcasters have public service obligations. They also serve the socially excluded directly since, although limited, they do have some spending power, and their high consumption of broadcasting means television advertising provides an effective way for advertisers to reach them. But there is a widespread expectation that the BBC, as the UK's primary public service broadcaster, should take the lead in serving the socially excluded.

6.5 In practical terms there are four main ways the BBC currently serves the socially excluded:

— providing a universal free-to-air service that generates a sense of inclusion;

— having a brand that the great majority of people value and trust, including the socially excluded, which means they share a common bond with wider society;

— offering value for money and an appropriate funding regime;

— running effective educational campaigns, often aimed at those who faired less well than others in formal learning environments.

The BBC has great strengths in all these areas, but there is always room for improvement.

6.6 Trends in technology and the move towards an information society are likely to change the way the BBC should serve the socially excluded.

— The BBC could use the concept of the 'digital dividend' and extend it to act as the 'Nation's Champion' in ensuring a universal service in the digital age.

— The BBC should battle to secure access for all in a new technological environment, make quality digital content a reality and build the BBC brand as a 'trusted friend'.

Chapter 1

Broadcasting Policy in the Multimedia Age

Andrew Graham[1]

1 Introduction

Digital technology is revolutionising broadcasting making possible multiple channels, interactivity, subscription TV and pay-per-view. Indeed, this change, occurring on a global scale, may well be the most significant development in communications since the introduction of the printing press by Gutenberg more than half a millennium ago.

The result is that broadcasting is moving rapidly into an apparently far more competitive and market driven environment. A central question for broadcasting policy in all countries is therefore how well this burgeoning (and converging) market will serve the public interest. The expansion of choice and the greater competition will be welcome, but will the market also foster a democratic environment, provide the information to which all citizens are entitled and extend, rather than diminish, the tastes, experiences and capacities of individuals? If not, how are these public interest goals to be achieved, especially in the more deregulated and more open environment that the global revolution in communications is producing? In short, what should broadcasting policy now be trying to do and how is this to be achieved?

2 The Fundamental Arguments

The best starting point for considering broadcasting policy is the claim that the new technology will allow television and radio programmes *to be made and sold in the market just like any other commodity and that this is desirable.* Note that this argument contains two separate propositions:

(a) that programmes *can* be sold commercially, and

(b) that it is *desirable* that this should occur.

Note also that the second does not automatically follow from the first. For

17

example, it is perfectly possible to buy and sell babies, but most of us find this morally repugnant and, at least in the UK, there are laws to prohibit it. This may seem an extreme case, but it should not be assumed that this makes it an isolated one. In reality there are many situations in which society aims to influence the market so that people buy less or more than would otherwise be the case. Thus society tries to ban some products all together (eg drugs or child pornography). In others it tries to limit consumption either via regulation (eg the distribution of alcohol) or through taxation (eg on tobacco). Society also influences consumption in a positive direction by promoting the use of some goods through laws (eg the requirement to wear seat belts) or by subsidies (eg grants to promote energy conservation) or by direct public provision (eg health care via the NHS).

The point about all these examples is that they remind us that, while the market functions extremely well for allocating some goods, it does *not* do so for all goods. The essential public policy question is therefore 'Does new technology make broadcasting just like many others goods that are sold successfully via the market or does it have any special characteristics which make this either impossible or undesirable?'

The case *in favour* of thinking that broadcasting is just like many other goods sold commercially was put forcibly by Peter Jay in evidence to the Peacock Committee in 1986. He regarded broadcasting in the age of new technology as simply 'electronic publishing'. He therefore argued that broadcasting, once it came fully of age, would require neither any public service presence nor any regulation save that of maintaining standards of taste and decency.[2]

In contrast, in what follows it will be shown that the goals that most people want from broadcasting will *not* be achieved by the market *on its own*. In particular we will argue that the way in which both the issue of choice and the analogies with publishing that have been formulated by Peacock and by almost everyone else who has followed these lines of argument are mistaken. As a result we shall show not only that a degree of regulation continues to be needed, but also that this regulation can be – and *needs* to be – complemented by an important component of public service broadcasting.

2.1 Policy implications

First, we show that, while the new technology undoubtedly makes possible many more channels as well as making it possible to sell individual programmes, that same technology also creates strong pressures towards a broadcasting industry in which *audiences are fragmented and yet whose ownership is concentrated*. Thus, instead of the appealing picture of free competition, there is a major danger of replacing public monopolies with private monopolies. Monopolies are *always* a matter for concern, but in a democratic society private monopolies in the media must be a matter for *special* concern.

Second, we give four sets of reasons why, even if the market in broadcasting were to be competitive, it would still be undesirable for *all* of broadcasting to be provided purely commercially. In brief these are:

- ## Market failure

  Economic analysis suggests strong grounds for thinking that private markets in broadcasting, good as they will be in some areas, will fail *on their own* to produce the *overall* quality of broadcasting that consumers either individually or collectively would desire. The two most important reasons why this happens are first, that broadcasting can have adverse 'external effects' (eg amplifying violence in society) and second, that good broadcasting is a 'merit' good (just as with education or training or checking on their health, consumers, if left to themselves tend to buy less than is in their own long term interests).

- ## Citizenship and community

  The market, being by definition the mere aggregation of individual decisions, takes no account of the community and of the complex relations between citizenship, culture and community. In particular, the fragmentation of audiences that pure market forces broadcasting may produce could undermine both communities and cultures by limiting our shared experiences.

- ## Democracy

  In a democratic society it is undesirable that the mass media should be entirely in private control (especially if such control were concentrated in few hands). Moreover, we show below that the creation and sustenance of 'common knowledge' (what everyone knows that everyone knows) is a vital element in the functioning of democracy and this 'common knowledge' is not well guarded by commercial markets.

- ## Industrial policy

  It is not the private market that has given the UK a broadcasting industry that is widely regarded as the best in the world. In the language of economists, by a clever mix of the public and the private, the UK has managed to generate for itself a 'comparative advantage' in broadcasting and it would be foolish now to throw this away.

Demonstrating that commercial broadcasting would fail in a variety of ways does not thereby establish that there should be public service broadcasting. It would still be possible, at least in principle, to regulate the market through a variety of rules. However, we show that, while some 'rules-based' interventions would be necessary, they would *not* be sufficient.

Most important of all, we show that in each of the four areas of concern public service broadcasting is a highly effective form of intervention. Moreover it is a form of intervention that achieves what regulation cannot. In particular, the direct provision of public service broadcasting creates the possibility for a *positive* influence on the system (filling gaps, setting standards, being universal and generating pressures towards high quality). As a result this achieves ends which rules, being by their very nature *negative*, never can. Finally, we demonstrate that technical change is making rules-based intervention *less* effective than in the past. Thus, the new technology increases, *not* decreases, the importance of public service broadcasting.

Finally, having established the case for public service broadcasting, the chapter concludes with a discussion of how such broadcasting should be financed.

3 The Effects of the New Technologies on Broadcasting

The usual argument about the new technology is that it will produce intense competition between delivery systems, between channels and between broadcasters. However, while it is correct that the number of *channels* will change in this way it does not follow that the number of *broadcasters* will change correspondingly. In reality it is far more likely both that broadcasting will remain highly concentrated in the hands of few large owners and that *particular* consumers will become reliant on a *single* supplier. If so, for these consumers, it will be as if they were able to shop at Tesco, but *only at Tesco*. The reasons why lie both with production and consumption.

3.1 Economies of scale

Take *production*: here two factors will generate highly concentrated broadcasting. First, both the making and broadcasting of radio and more especially television programmes has exceptionally high fixed costs. At the same time they have very low, in many cases zero, marginal costs. Almost by definition, to 'broadcast' is to say that it costs no more to reach extra people. Economists describe this phenomenon as either 'economies of scale' or as the gap between 'first copy' and 'second copy'. When economies of scale are significant (ie when this gap is large), entry to the market is difficult and firms tend to be concentrated.

Against this some argue that the new technology is lowering entry costs and that the market will therefore become more competitive. With one exception, the Internet (considered further below), this is much less so than, at first, it seems. Admittedly the digital revolution is making cameras and recording equipment much smaller and in some cases cheaper (or more sophisticated for the same price). New technology has also allowed much simpler, and so faster, processing and editing. Nevertheless the fundamental point is that most costs are not equipment but people – and not just individual people, but *teams* of people (writers, designers, performers, etc) all working together. In aggregate these are considerable – especially for programmes of any quality. In 1998 the *average* cost per hour of a BBC production was £120,000 on BBC One and £80,000 on BBC Two; a current affairs programme approximately £154,000 and drama programmes approach half a million. Typical ITV costs were £95,000 per hour. Similarly the fixed costs of transmission, whether in renting space on satellites, or in establishing digital terrestrial broadcasting facilities, or in installing fibre optic cables to the home, rule out all except the very large.

Most important is that the real cost of the *content* of quality programmes is rising not falling. All the discussion of technical change in the delivery of programmes ignores the fact that *talent and desirable content is scarce.* Moreover, it is the technical change in delivery that is bringing this scarcity to the fore. The combination of more channels with multimedia companies that are increasingly operating on a global basis is generating far greater competition for services that are in short supply. In effect an economic rent (a payment for scarcity) which in the past was suppressed by the bargaining power of the small number of broadcasters is now being revealed. The result is that in the last six years up to 1996 the average cost of the top 100 contributors to UK television rose *in real terms* by nearly 7 per cent per annum (or by more than 50 per cent in total) and, on average, the total talent costs for sitcoms, drama, features and documentaries rose by approximately 5 per cent per annum in real terms.[3]

Sports rights illustrate the problem even more dramatically. Formula 1 Grand Prix which cost the BBC £2 million per annum during the years 1993-96 was sold to ITV in 1997 for more than seven times that sum. Similarly, at the start of the 1990s, premier league football was costing ITV some £12 million per annum. 10 years later similar rights will be costing Sky and the BBC more than £170 million per annum. In the face of such figures it is hard to take seriously the idea that broadcasting can be a world of small competitors.

3.2 *Economies of scope*

The second factor generating concentration is that, in addition to economies of scale, the new technology creates what economists call 'economies of scope'. Such economies occur when activities in one area either decrease costs or increase revenues in a second area. New technology (in particular the digitalisation of all information and the convergence that this is making possible) is greatly increasing this. For example, in the past newspapers and television stations were separate activities. Today, information gathered for a newspaper can be repackaged as a radio or television programme. Indeed, because digital information can be endlessly edited, copied, stored, retrieved, redesigned and merged with other information it can reappear in a multiplicity of formats. In short, the very same technology that *removes* spectrum scarcity *creates* concentration.

Strong evidence that economies of scope plus scarcity of good content will produce concentration of ownership can already be seen. In particular, the digital revolution and the convergence it is creating are a major cause of the extraordinary global rush to multimedia mergers observed in recent years. Every one of the top seven multimedia firms in the world has in the last few years been buying, merging or being bought.

So powerful are the pressures towards convergence that even companies quite outside the multimedia world have been buying in. Seagram (the world's second largest distiller) bought MCA from Matsushita in 1995 for just under $6 billion and in 1998 is set to complete its purchase of Polygram for $10 billion. In 1995 Westinghouse, primarily an electrical goods company, bought CBS for $5.4 billion and in 1996 bid $3.7 billion for Infinity Broadcasting. Similarly Proctor and Gamble (best known as makers of detergents) has formed a strategic alliance with Paramount Television (owned by Viacom).[4]

Also relevant is that the scale of these global mergers is considerably greater than that of even the largest UK multimedia firms. Time Warner or Disney or Bertelsmann all have turnovers that are five times or more larger than the BBC and ten to twenty times larger than the Mirror Group. Concentration of ownership is therefore already a fact not a speculation.

3.3 Delivery systems and gateways

Now consider *delivery*. It is clear here that the new technology is increasing the number of ways by which broadcasting can be delivered (by satellite by cable and by telephone lines). In addition, digital technology means that the number of channels that can be carried by *each* of these means is also rising. Indeed in the digital world the concept of the channel might seem to be redundant – there is just a stream of bits which are first one programme and then another. At first glance competition in delivery therefore appears to be a real possibility.

In practice, however, the very technology that makes competition look likely also creates the conditions for proprietary control. The area of greatest concern is the set-top box through which cable and satellite signals pass at the moment and through which in the future *all* digital signals will have to pass. Moreover digital technology will allow these gateways to be quite sophisticated. Once 'channels', in the old sense, disappear, the gateway will be the means by which consumers select programmes (using what are called Electronic Programme Guides, EPGs). But these EPGs will do far more than select. They will work in conjunction with other software and hardware known as the Applications Programming Interface (API). The result will be to make the television much more like a computer – for the first time televisions will have 'operating systems'. These will not only define how data and interactive services will look and operate, they will also soon allow access to a variety of 'smart' features, such as automatically recording particular programmes, or finding programmes of a particular type and alerting the viewer.

What seems almost inevitable in these circumstances is that any one consumer will only be willing to buy a single box. What is more, if there are rival boxes on sale (as looks likely in the UK at the moment with the battle between ONdigital and Sky Digital), one will eventually capture the market. The analogy with VHS and Betamax makes the point. If so, then, despite the increase in the number of delivery systems, there will only be a single point through which every digital channel from every broadcaster has to pass. Certainly, except for the very rich, any one consumer will be entirely dependent on the box of one proprietor.

Moreover, this question of the control of the gateway is not just a matter of technical interest. Anyone who controls the gateway also, at least in principle, has the power to control the agenda. The way the EPG is designed will influence what you see when you first switch on, where it is easiest to go next, what is drawn to your attention (and what is not) and what your TV goes to as its 'default' setting. Such gateways could also be used to control a service provider's ability to access the viewer. These are, of course, precisely the issues over which Microsoft has been taken to court in the USA – its browser is to the Internet what the EPG/API will be to digital television.

3.4 The Internet

So far it has been argued that the characteristics of production, content and delivery all suggest strong underlying pressures towards concentration and monopolisation. However, today's Information Superhighway (in the shape of the Internet) appears to offer a counter example. Millions of people are placing information on it every day and even greater millions are using it to retrieve information. Leaving the issue of browsers on one side, it is therefore not at all monopolised. *However, far from this being counter evidence, this is – at least so far – the exception that proves the rule.*

The Internet is not monopolised for three key reasons. First, the system was developed primarily by University research workers[5] totally committed to creating an open system – the whole philosophy of the Internet is that it should be capable of connecting to all systems anywhere. Second, until 1994 academic users predominated and entry for them was particularly easy as most of them have their fixed costs supported by public funding. Third, and most important, the majority of the content on the Internet is extremely cheap to produce. This is because the cost of collecting certain kinds of information (most obviously personal information or personally created information) is very low, and because, psychologically, people appear to value self-promotion and/or participation (so labour costs are zero). But, and this is also central, being cheap, much of the content available on the Internet is of abysmal quality.

Of course there is some good material on the Internet, but most of the material that is better quality is there either because it has been well organised to attract advertising, or because it has been produced by public or quasi-public bodies (universities, libraries, museums, etc). Much of the rest is poor precisely because it is cheap and because they lack the implicit codes of professionalism that characterise existing reputable sources of information. Indeed even the British Government fails in many cases to say when the information was first posted or when it was last revised. A great deal of the information on today's Information Highway is therefore misleading or hard to understand.

In short, the great majority of the Internet is at the opposite end of the spectrum from mass market, high quality, multimedia broadcasting. In the digital age both the Internet and traditional broadcasting can, *just*, be described as 'electronic publishing', but this catch-all phrase fails to draw the following important distinction. On one hand we have material that is personally addressable, usually received in private, is low cost and frequently low quality. On the other hand we have material that is broadcast to a mass market, often received in public and which, if it is to be of high quality, will have high fixed costs. Of course there are already intermediate cases (such as CD-ROMs) and the new technology will spawn more, many more, but to say that we cannot therefore distinguish one from the other is as unhelpful as saying that because night shades imperceptibly into day we do not know the difference.

3.5 Dilemmas for public policy: concentration and fragmentation

The central point, true both of today's broadcasting and tomorrow's Information Superhighway, is that *high* quality multimedia content is expensive to produce in the first place and yet, once commissioned and created, is relatively cheap to edit or to change and trivially cheap to reproduce. In other words, as already stated, it has high fixed costs and low marginal costs – and these are the natural creators of monopolies.

Here we have a critical dilemma for public policy. High quality material can still be produced and yet cost very little *per unit* provided that it reaches a large number of people (exploiting economies of scale) and/or provided that it is used in a wide variety of different formats (exploiting economies of scope). However, the exploitation of these economies of scale and scope imply concentration of ownership. Thus, even though the new technology has removed one source of monopoly, spectrum scarcity, it has replaced it with another, the natural monopoly of economies of scale.

How then should this potential concentration be tackled? Can it be left to the market or does it have to be regulated (or influenced) in one way or another, and, if so, how? We return to these questions below.

Another dilemma follows logically from the combination of economies of scale and scope on the one hand and a constrained audience on the other. More channels have *not* meant more time is being spent watching television. In 1995 in the UK on average each person watched TV for twenty-five hours per week. This is *identical* to what it was in 1980 before the arrival of either Channel 4, or cable or satellite. Thus more channels fragment audiences. The inevitable consequence is that the audience per channel or per programme falls and, given economies of scale, the average cost rises. This is *not* true for most goods and services that are allocated via the market place. A larger choice of restaurants or shoe shops or hotels does not lead to higher costs, in fact frequently the opposite as competition pushes costs down. The difference between these goods and services and broadcasting is that the former have much smaller fixed costs and variable costs are also significant. Thus minimum cost production is quite small, whereas minimum cost production in broadcasting is large. The result is that *choice has a cost in broadcasting* and this is a cost that is *not* normally faced elsewhere. Under 'free market' conditions consumers will face a choice between a narrower range of cheaper (and yet still high quality) broadcasting and a broader range of more expensive and yet lower quality programmes.

The obvious response from those who advocate the expansion of commercial TV is that this is a choice that should be left to consumers. Why do otherwise? If some consumers want lots of choice and the consequence is that they pay more and yet, on average, receive lower quality, is that not up to them and does the market not correctly reflect their wishes? Surprising as it may seem, analysis suggests the opposite.

The reason that the individual choices via the market do not capture individual's wishes accurately is because of 'externalities'. These are the effects of one person's purchase on someone else, but which the market ignores. The effects may be either harmful, as in the case of traffic congestion arising from private car use, or beneficial as in the case of vaccinations – everyone benefits from the fact that *other* people are vaccinated. The existence of externalities means that left to itself the market produces too many car journeys and too few vaccinations (which is one reason why petrol is taxed particularly heavily and why there are public health programmes for vaccinations).

In the case being examined here the externalities arise because the person who migrates away from existing channels in favour of others imposes a cost on all those who do not move. This is a cost that the mover does not have to pay. Indeed the mover is not even aware of any cost so s/he does not take into account. The situation is analogous to that of membership of a club. Clubs have common facilities, the costs of which have to be shared. As a result, if someone leaves all the remaining members face either higher charges or worse facilities or both. But this is not the optimal outcome. If the members who remain were able to organise

25

themselves they would all be willing to offer the potential leaver a sum just below the extra costs that they would otherwise face in order to try the persuader to remain. If such 'side payments' were on offer fewer people would decide to leave. However, in broadcasting it is impossible to organise in this way because it is too expensive to find them and to communicate with them (they are numerous, unknown and unreachable). As a result a pure free market in broadcasting would be biased in favour of too much fragmentation of audiences (and, at the same time, too much concentration of ownership).

4 Other Market Failures in Broadcasting

4.1 Consumers and market failure

There is another set of `externalities' which applies to broadcasting more than most other goods and services. These are not the direct result of fragmentation, but, like excessive fragmentation, they also threaten quality. These exist once we suppose, as both common sense and research suggests (a) that television has some influence upon the lifestyles, habits, interests, etc, of those who watch it and (b) that these habits and interests have implications for those around us. Indeed, even just the *belief* that television affects behaviour is sufficient for externalities to exist. An elderly person may become more fearful of walking down the street at night if they believe that the portrayal of large amounts of irrational violence on TV encourages such behaviour, irrespective of whether in fact it does or not. The possible falseness of the belief does not alter the genuineness of the fear. In other words the television that is broadcast ought to reflect the preferences not only of those who watch it but also those affected by it indirectly – yet the market cannot do this. It follows that, if left just to the market, more 'bad' TV (bad in the sense of being judged to have harmful side effects) and less 'good' TV will be purchased than consumers in aggregate would have wished if they could have acted collectively.

A further reason why a broadcasting market would not work as well as that for many other goods and services is that markets do not work well where what is being sold is information or experience. People do not know what they are 'buying' until they have experienced it, yet once they have experienced it they no longer need to buy it! Of course it can be argued that in such information-based markets consumers are often willing to experiment by paying for the right to access a bundle of information with the chance that some might prove useful. But this argument does not remove the problem. If the right long-run choices are to be made, the cost of the initial experiments should only be the marginal cost of disseminating the information, and in the case of broadcasting this is zero.[6]

Third, and most important, the theory of choice on which the *economic* claim in favour of a free market in broadcasting rests relies on a fallacious assumption. This theory assumes that consumers *already* know their own preferences. Indeed it operates *as if* people arrive in the world *already* fully formed. Strictly speaking, such an assumption is false everywhere. Nevertheless, after a period of time, it may be a reasonable assumption for some goods and services – people undoubtedly do have different tastes and they can *find out* by experiment what meets their tastes. However, in broadcasting such an assumption is *seriously* flawed. Much of broadcasting exists to inform and educate us, but the process of learning and understanding the world is part of how our preferences are *formed*. They cannot therefore be taken as given in advance.

Those who advocate a free market in broadcasting discount both this and the preceding argument (about the costs of information) on the grounds that television unlike, say, a pension policy, is purchased every day, so any mistakes that a consumer may make can be quickly corrected. That much is true, but what is at issue here is both subtler and more important. The point is that in the particular case of broadcasting, consumers may be unavoidably myopic about their own long-term interests. Consumers cannot be other than ill informed about effects that broadcasting may have on them, *including effects on their preferences about television itself*. Moreover, such effects may well be spread out over a period of years after the reception of the broadcasts.

The point being made here is not that television may have great power for good or evil over society as a whole, but that television has the capacity either to cramp or to expand the knowledge, experience and imagination of *individuals*. Television fictions, for example, '...can expand the viewer's sense of what is possible and enhance his or her vocabularies and repertoires of words, gestures and initiatives... *only if they are of high quality*' (emphasis added).[7] In other words, if all programmes are elicited by the market, there is a very real danger that consumers will under-invest in the *development* of their *own* tastes, their *own* experience and their *own* capacity to comprehend. This is not because consumers are stupid but because it is only in retrospect that the benefits of such investment may become apparent.[8]

In technical terms, good quality broadcasting is what economists call a 'merit good'. It is analogous to eating sensibly or receiving preventative health care. No matter how much someone tells us in advance that we need it, the evidence is that, in general, we under-invest in it. In a free market in broadcasting where each item would have to be paid for at the point of use, this tendency to under-invest in watching those programmes which did not attract us at that moment would be greatly (and mistakenly) increased.

The arguments above have focused on how, seen from the standpoint of the *consumer*, a pure market in broadcasting would have some drawbacks – possibly quite severe. Moreover, these concerns become larger when seen in the context of how the producers of broadcasting might behave.

4.2 Market failures in production

The danger that market driven broadcasting will lead to concentration on the side of production has already been discussed, but there are two more general problems. First, it is well recognized by economists that pure market economies will under invest in training. This is because each firm tends to free ride, buying in talent when it needs it. Such behavior is rational for each firm, but not for the system as a whole. Second, there is some evidence that in countries such as the USA and the UK, which have highly developed financial markets, that firms take too 'short' a view, have not innovated sufficiently, and have given insufficient attention to quality. The explanation of these failings is complex, but one factor suggested in research is the structure of these financial markets places an undue premium on corporate control. The result is that USA and UK firms are forced to pay higher dividends than their competitors abroad in order to resist the threat of take-over and that these high payouts reduce investment.

The changes that have occurred in broadcasting in the 1980s and 1990s illustrate the problem. At the start of the 1980s the ITV companies had a narrow and, typically, privately controlled share ownership. But, since the Broadcasting Act of 1981, their share ownership has been widened and they are now traded on the stock exchange. The result has been a much sharper conflict than in the past between, on the one hand, the quasi-public service obligations placed on them first by the IBA and later by the ITC and, on the other hand, the need to generate cash flow and to increase dividends.

In the UK the existence of public service broadcasters (PSBs) has gone some way to solve both of these market failures – at least in the case of broadcasting. In the case of training, in particular, the PSBs have acted as a 'talent-conveyor' belts, attracting many of the best staff early in their careers, training them well and then allowing the benefits of this training to spread throughout the broadcasting industry. The BBC has also been able to invest for the longer term and, since 1982, the operation of the system has been further helped by the existence of Channel 4. Here, too, explicit public service obligations, together with guaranteed income for several years, have encouraged C4 to take a longer view than the market would allow. This room for manoeuvre, plus a remit which explicitly requires C4 to innovate and to provide programmes calculated to appeal to tastes and interests not generally catered for by ITV, has again extended consumers tastes in ways that many denied were possible in advance.

4.3 Market failure: the interaction of consumption and production

The possibility of a purely commercial broadcasting market failing to provide what individuals in society ultimately want is still more worrying when the interaction of production with consumption is considered. If prices are higher (because of fragmentation) and consumers prove unwilling to pay the prices that good programmes require (because they underestimate the benefits of 'good' programmes) then broadcasters will not have the incentive to invest in producing such programmes. Conversely, if broadcasters are not providing good programmes, even well informed and far-sighted consumers cannot buy them. To this may be added the possible external effects from one broadcaster to another via the consumer: each broadcaster may well consider his own (good) programme not commercially worthwhile unless other broadcasters are also transmitting good programmes that are gradually extending consumers' tastes. Putting it bluntly, we will be 'dumbed down' as the Americans say.

These theoretical concerns find support in practice both from experience abroad and from the history of broadcasting in the UK. Admittedly, there is, as yet, little *direct* evidence on exactly how a fully commercial system based largely on pay-TV would operate as no country has such a system. Even those with pay-TV and dominated by commercial sectors gain by far the greatest part of their revenue from advertising. Nevertheless, the inferences that can be drawn are not encouraging. Other countries with a low element of public service broadcasting typically display poor quality, concentration of ownership plus frequent battles over ownership, flouting of regulators' rules and more or less subtle forms of government interference.

In France, for example, the *Financial Times* described the effects of deregulation as having heralded 'an anarchic scenario of dozens of different channels pumping out soft porn and pulp programming punctuated by virtually unrestricted advertising'.[9] Experience in Germany and Italy offers similar warnings. German pay-TV appears to contain large amounts of pornography. In Italy, on the face of it there is intense competition with well over 30 local channels. However, in practice, they are virtually all controlled by Fininvest, owned by Silvio Berlusconi, and the Fininvest channels have been much criticised for their down-market programming (consisting of some 90 per cent of entertainment and with over 50 per cent of total programming imported from the USA).

The case of the USA is the most interesting as the US has the largest commercial broadcasting market in the world both absolutely and proportionately. Here the move from a system with a small number of channels almost all financed by advertising to a multiplicity of channels and an expansion of pay-TV (both subscription and per programme) has genuinely extended choice. It has increased diversity, provided more and better news coverage and extended significantly the range of sports, music, language, educational, weather, travel and other special interest channels.[10]

This is what one would expect. Advertising inevitably concentrates on the mass, middle income, market. Audience size, not how much the audience values the programme, is what matters. In addition, as channels multiply the

29

incentive to look at minority interests rises. When there are only two channels they will each locate near the middle of the market and try to acquire fifty one per cent of it, whereas when there are, say, ten channels it becomes worthwhile to focus on a group that only constitutes ten per cent of the population. Television financed by pay per view is therefore far better than television financed by advertising at reflecting consumer wants.

Such observations, showing an improvement over time within the USA, are not, however, at odds with the argument above that a purely market driven system will fail in important ways. While the US market undoubtedly offers considerable choice, few would say that it offers television of such high quality as that of the UK, Australian or Canada, where there has been a much stronger contribution by PSBs. 'Dumbing down', to use that USA term again, seems frequently to be the only concern.

We must also remember that the US is a special situation. As a result of its vast market it faces less of a problem from the higher unit costs that accompany a proliferation of channels. In the USA channels can increase and yet the audience size per channel can still be high, so the trade-off between choice and quality is less severe than for countries with smaller audiences. Moreover, even with such a large market it has only relatively recently begun to develop its own significant original productions for the cable channels and its public service broadcasting (reaching only about three per cent of the audience) have had to rely heavily in the past on importing programmes made abroad (especially from the UK).

More serious is that the USA provides little good broadcasting for children and what there is relies on advertising, or, worse still, on *insidious* advertising either via 'infomercials' or by producing shows based on a toy (eg 'Care Bears', 'He Man', 'Transformers', 'GoBots' and 'Masters of the Universe').[11] As Noam comments, 'The most successful channel for children is Viacom's Nickelodeon, which has 30 per cent of the viewing time of 6-11 year olds .... its programmes are more entertaining than educational.' The USA is also thought to have provided only a 'continuing narrow scope for political information'.[12]

UK experience, in contrast, with a strong public service presence and ethos is widely acknowledged to have much good quality broadcasting and to have raised the quality over time. In his study of broadcasting in the 1980s Tim Madge refers to the extent to which the television programme-makers have enhanced the sophistication of their audiences so that '... programmes are made which simply could not have been "read" correctly a few years ago'.[13]

4.4 The company you keep

These points about quality can be made another way. In many aspects of our lives we readily recognise that the environment within which we live and the people with whom we work can have an enormous influence on what we do, or do not, achieve. To take just a few examples: everyone wants children to go to high quality schools, or sports people to have the best coaches, or firms to learn from best practice world-wide. Yet is not television part of the company we all keep? Including radio, the BBC estimate that the average household spends more than a quarter of all their leisure time watching or listening to the BBC. Moreover, children watch it more than the average. So also do adults who have children. It is impossible to measure what effects this has since it is not possible to run the experiment of what society without television would be like. Nevertheless it is inconceivable that it has anything other than a powerful effect.

A more specific example of the importance of 'the company you keep'[14] is the imaginative, creative and lively character of much UK TV advertising. Being sandwiched between programmes that are themselves, in general, well made and imaginative is undoubtedly part of the reason. The advertisers have been put on their toes and have responded – and, no doubt, some of the effects also run the other way. The important point is that each has stretched the other and so each has achieved more – and this has *not* been a pure market outcome.

5 Citizenship, Culture and Community

The argument, so far, has been that there is a case for public service broadcasting so as to make good the deficiencies of the market in providing what well informed *consumers*, acting either individually or in aggregate, would wish to buy over the longer term. A quite separate argument arises from the fact that there are parts of our lives to which the market is simply not relevant. To be more concrete, we watch television and listen to the radio, not just as consumers, but also as *citizens*.

Our citizenship carries with it three separate implications. First, as citizens we have rights. This includes the right to certain core information about our own society. Thus almost everyone would agree that anyone is entitled to know *without having to pay for it* such basic things as the key items of news, their legal rights, who their MP is, etc. It is immediately obvious that the market makes no provision for this (any more than it does for basic education or primary health care for the poor). In this new context the informational role of a public service broadcaster, operating universally, is therefore more important than ever. As the local public library declines, so the ever present public broadcaster must fill the gap – and for zero charge at the margin.

Second, as citizens we have views about society that cannot be captured just in our buying and selling. In particular in a wide ranging investigation carried out in 1994 and 1995 the Bertelsmann Foundation working with the European Institute for the Media found that in all ten countries covered people expected and wanted 'socially responsible television'.[15] Moreover, they concluded, 'responsibility in programming has a chance only if and when it has been defined and constantly pursued as a strategic aim in the management [of the broadcaster]'.[16] It is difficult to see how both profitability and responsibility can be constant strategic aims at the same

31

time. In the competitive market place profitability is bound to take priority.

Third, as citizens we are members of a community. It has been said that while we are all individual we are also all individual *somebodies*. In other words our sense of our own identity derives from how we see ourselves in relation to society and from where we 'locate' ourselves within it. Stated simply, there is intrinsic value to individuals if they have a sense of community – to be alienated is literally to lose a part of oneself.

The crucial importance of broadcasting in this context is that for the great majority of people it is today their major source of information about the world, beyond that of family, friends and acquaintances. Television provides not only the hard facts, but also the fuzzy categories – the social, ethnic, psychological, etc, concepts within which we must make sense of the world. It also supplies a set of fantasies, emotions and fictional images with which we construct our understanding (or misunderstanding) of all those parts of society beyond our immediate surroundings. It is therefore part not just of how we see ourselves in relation to the community, or communities, within which we are embedded, but also part of how we understand the community – indeed part of where the very idea of community arises and is given meaning.

This is true as much of low as of high culture. The latest episode of a soap opera or a recent football match can function as a topic upon which all members of the society can form an opinion or converse with one another regardless of the differences in their life-style or social class. Since all societies contain such differences, the value of a community where people have things in common and can interact on that basis is, or should be, obvious.

The value of commonality, the value of shared experience, the value of self-identity and the value provided by non-stereotypical portrayal of other cultures are not considerations that do, or could, enter into the transactions of the market place – but they are values nonetheless. For all of these reasons there is a case for a public service broadcaster, one of whose objectives would be the provision of those broadcasts to which we are entitled as citizens. Moreover, a genuinely national public service broadcaster could provide the material for such commonality in ways that other broadcasting organisations, with a less extensive and penetrating reach, could not match.

5.1 Fragmentation

This general point about commonality takes on added importance as well as a different form in the context of a pluralist society, such as Britain in the late 1990s. Traditional forms of social unity are widely believed to be breaking down. Alongside this, new sub-cultures based on, for example, religion, race, sexual orientation and so on, proliferate. If, at the same time, there were to be a wholly 'free market' in broadcasting based on an abundance of channels, this would itself fragment audiences and, by so doing, increase the sense of separateness. In such a context, the risks of socio-cultural misunderstandings are high. By the same token the value of any medium by means of which that fragmentation could be combated is increased.

The importance of a public service broadcaster in this process would not be to promote a single culture. Instead its role would be to broadcasting informed and accurate representations of minority cultures. By so doing it would help to maintain, across these different cultures, a shared emphasis upon respect for human life. Moreover, the extent and penetration of a national broadcaster would be both a requirement and a significant advantage; for in modern society, one of the main ways of legitimising a given sub-culture is by conferring a public profile upon through television.

5.2 National events

The final area under the heading of citizenship and community where a public service broadcaster should be expected to play a special role is in the broadcasting of National Events. Here, the idea would be that a public service broadcaster should be given the responsibility to broadcast events which are of genuinely national interest. The events in question would include happenings anywhere in the world that are of general significance (eg the collapse of the Berlin Wall), or to this country in particular (eg the UK athletics team in the Olympic Games), as well as events in the UK that are primarily of importance to its citizens (eg the resignation of a Prime Minister, Royal weddings or European and General Elections). The idea would not be to stop the commercial stations covering such events, but to ensure (especially as we move into pay-per-view) that events which are constitutive of citizenship are also available free at the point of view. Such broadcasting service would help to maintain a sense of national identity, which transcends more local communal identifications and allows individuals to understand themselves as members of a particular nation. And a public service broadcaster's relative advantage here would derive from its experience and expertise at performing such functions, together with its capacity for genuinely national dissemination.

6 Democracy and the Mass Media

It is a basic principle of a democratic society that votes should not be bought and sold. 'Candidates should be able to talk to voters on the strengths of their ideas, not their [wallets]'.[17] This alone is sufficient justification for broadcasting not being entirely commercial. It is, by the same token, the major reason why broadcasting should not be directly under the control of the State. There has to be a source of information, which can be trusted to be accurate in its news, documentaries and current affairs programmes, and to be impartial between different social and political views. It is a necessary, but not sufficient condition, for this to be possible that some at least of the broadcasters be independent of any political party and of any business interest.

In the late 1990s there are good grounds for thinking that the need for a public service broadcaster to exist and to uphold the principles of truth and impartiality will be even greater than in the past. Two factors in particular stand out. First, the media is today most people's main source of information for anything beyond that of work and home. Second, there will soon be many more purveyors of information – of hard news, soft news, of fact and of faction.

It is not enough, however, for truth to be upheld. It must also be available – and available to all. The advantages of the BBC (and to a similar but lesser extent, Channel 4) in these circumstances are clear. They have national scope and are easily accessible. Moreover, the BBC in particular has a worldwide reputation, which provides the basis for trust without which much information is just propaganda. In addition, its independence from both Government and commercial or market-place pressures has made it more capable of representing unpopular or otherwise unpalatable truths. These arguments are not, however, absolute ones, but contingent upon behaviour. While the BBC's reputation is mostly deserved, there have been times when it has been justifiably criticised for being too much under the influence of the Government. Moreover, a number of supposedly 'public service' broadcasters in other countries have been little more than mouthpieces for the State. It follows that the reputation of the BBC has to continue to be *earned*.

It should also not be assumed (as it often is) that commercial broadcasting is necessarily *freer* of politics than public service broadcasting just because one is public and one is commercial. In France there were close connections between Canal Plus and Mitterrand. In Italy the interventions have been far more blatant with Berlusconi using his TV stations to support both his political position and his business interests.

6.1 Common knowledge

So far the arguments about the relationship between the mass media and democracy strongly reinforce the case for public service broadcasters existing as major sources of independent, accurate and impartial information. However, such ideas need to be seen in a wider context. Although it is not often recognised, society depends critically on the existence of 'common knowledge'[18] – what everybody knows that everybody knows. Most of the time the existence of such knowledge is taken for granted. However, it plays a role in society that is both more profound and more important than at first it seems.

The influence of common knowledge is more profound than it might seem because *any* debate requires *some* common knowledge – as a minimum, it has to be agreed what is being debated. Moreover, in modern societies the media is one major way in which common knowledge is *created*. It is also more important than it might seem because almost all solutions to problems require the *extension* of common knowledge. In order to be *agreed,* solutions have to be based on a common understanding of the situation. Common knowledge is therefore a *pre-condition* of many co-ordination problems in democratic societies.

Agreeing on solutions and agreeing on *correct* solutions are not, however, the same thing. Or to put the same point another way, knowledge, which implies that what is known is true, is not the same as belief, which may or may not be true. The 'power of the witchdoctor' may have been thought of as common knowledge, but strictly speaking it was only 'common belief'. Another more contemporary example which displays both the power of the media and the danger and inefficiency of inaccurate 'common knowledge', if we may use that contradiction, comes from the experience reported by the Labour MP, Dianne Abbott. When visiting a London school she asked what number the pupils would dial in an emergency. The answer from many was '911' – the US emergency number!

This example also illustrates that 'knowledge' and 'information' need to be understood as including much more than is dealt with by news programmes. Every kind of programme is a contributor to the concepts and images of everyday discourse.

Furthermore, central to the idea of the democratic society is that of the well-informed and self-determining individual; but, if individuals are to be genuinely autonomous, it is not sufficient for them merely to receive information (no matter how much and how impartially presented), they must be able to *understand* it. They must be able to make sense of it in ways that relate to their own lives and decisions. Information without 'organising insights' is just noise.

The media has therefore a double responsibility. First, programmes need to handle information in such a way that it increases understanding and creates knowledge. Second, programmes need to ensure, as far as possible, that such knowledge correctly represents the world. This is not something restricted to the domain of news or documentaries. In the UK the strong tradition of public service broadcasting means that, in general, talk show hosts act responsibly. Thus blatantly inaccurate comments, for example about how many immigrants there have been, would typically be challenged. This is far from the case in countries where commercial interests predominate. In 1996 the New York radio station WABC fired a talk show host called Bob Grant, but this was only after twenty-five years of regular attacks on blacks, Hispanics and other minorities. An ABC producer commented that 'Our advertisers are aware that hate sells their products'.[19]

The editorial responsibility that is so obviously lacking in this case is not surprising. If the product sells and makes a profit that is all that is required. Ethical judgements, even where the only ethical requirement is a respect for evidence, is not part of its natural domain. Its *purpose* is to make money, not to sustain democracy, nor to expand common knowledge nor to extend the tastes and capacities of its audience.

Purposes matter. Almost all societies allow children to attend a single school for many years. The school is therefore the monopoly provider of both information and understanding – and at a particularly formative stage in a person's life. Yet an equivalent commercial monopoly, even later in life, is strongly resisted. The reason is that schools and commerce have different objectives. The *purpose* of a school is not to indoctrinate, but to educate. Indeed the exception proves the rule. In the rare number of cases when people do object to the influence of schools it is usually because the school is suspected of peddling a particular point of view to the detriment of education. The *purpose* of educators is to empower other people and they want to teach people what questions to ask and how to use information to understand the world. Such an assumption cannot be made of the commercial world. The purpose of the commercial world is to make a profit. Nothing wrong in that, but it is different.

In brief, if democracy and the role of its citizens are left just to the market, they will be poorly served. There will be a gap in broadcasting, which, in a fully functioning democracy, requires public service broadcasting to fill it. Moreover one key principle for public service broadcasters to follow on this count is that they should aim to extend the understanding and experience of those who watch or listen.

Public service broadcasters performing this function would therefore provide a central forum – the public space – within which society could engage in the process of extending its common knowledge as well as in illuminating and either re-affirming, questioning or extending its already-existing values.

7 Industrial Policy

One final argument against relying entirely on the market remains. The countries which have performed best at producing programmes the rest of the world wants to see and hear have not been those dominated either by commercial broadcasting or by state run broadcasting, but those in which there has been a powerful public service tradition (suitably distanced from Government) combined with a commercial sector. The UK and to a lesser extent Australia are the two prime examples. The USA has, of course, been dominant in the audio-visual industry, but this has been because of its power in films (derived from the dominance of Hollywood), *not* because of its television or radio. Equally few would look to Italy or France where state influence in broadcasting has been far too excessive to allow creative ideas to flourish.

The UK's success has been led by the BBC and is the result of extensive investment in talent over many years. The result is that the BBC has developed a *comparative advantage*. No amount of abstract theorising justifies throwing success away. It would be even more foolish to duplicate (or to try to duplicate) in other broadcasting organisations identical strengths to those that the BBC already possesses – the attempt would probably damage both the old and the new (the remit for Channel 4 carefully avoided making this mistake).

Many of the areas in which the BBC probably has a comparative advantage have, of course, emerged purely contingently through historical commitments. For example, the BBC has long-standing connections with specific events and areas of programming (eg the Proms, Wimbledon, coronations, music, sport, nature programmes, news and current affairs). In some of these areas it is likely that through the process of 'learning by doing' the BBC has developed genuine advantages quite irrespective of its particular concerns as a public service broadcaster. Where the BBC has such an advantage, but only where it has such advantage, the accumulated experience, expertise, economies of scale and intimacy with the relevant organisational bodies should be capitalised upon, not ignored nor regarded as optional.

Of course there is a danger that this argument could be misused, being deployed as a defence of everything that the BBC now does, but this is not the intention at all. The point is a simple one. Activities that the market might support should not be stripped away from the BBC just because it is a public broadcaster. Equally, activities that the market might handle better should not be left with the BBC just because they have been with the BBC in the past. The decision should be pragmatic not ideological.

8 Rules-Based Intervention versus Public Service Broadcasting

We have established, so far, a *prima facie* case for intervention, but such arguments provide no guidance on the *form* that intervention should take. Why could market failures not be dealt with by regulation as occurs, for example, in the case of health and safety legislation?

Our answer to this question is in two parts. First, we agree that in some cases regulation *is* appropriate. For example, if the *only* concern of public policy were that child pornography should not be broadcast then rules banning this activity would make an important contribution. However, our second answer is far more important. We consider that in the particular case of broadcasting, rules-based intervention is necessary but *not* sufficient, especially in the new environment of the 1990s.

The first reason why rules are insufficient is that many of the issues concerning broadcasting are qualitative rather than quantitative in nature. This is self-evidently true of quality itself, but it applies equally to the discussion above of the importance of maintaining a sense of community as well as valuing a democratic society. These broad principles which should guide part of broadcasting could not be incorporated in any *precise* set of rules – indeed it is the impossibility of doing so that differentiates qualitative from quantitative assessments.

The second reason why rules are insufficient is that rules are, at best, negative – especially when regulating *against* strong commercial forces. While regulation may, therefore, be able to protect standards, for example by *preventing* the display of excessive violence or sexual material considered offensive, it is much less well suited to *promoting* quality.

This point is central. At numerous points above it has been shown that *purposes* matter. But purposes are about *doing* things – educating, informing and entertaining, for example. Such purposes cannot possibly be achieved by rules because rules cannot make things happen. This is of great importance because, in the case of broadcasting we have shown that there are gaps in the system which require *positive* pressure to correct them. This is why, corresponding to each area in which the market would fall down, it has been possible above to identify one or more primary *objectives* that a public service broadcaster should pursue. To offset market failure it should aim to expand quality and to extend individuals ideas of what they can achieve; to meet the requirements of citizenship it should provide for the needs of community (or communities); to sustain democracy it should extend common knowledge and empower those that watch it or listen to it; and in industrial policy PSBs should concentrate on those areas in which they have already established a comparative advantage.

Moreover, none of these objectives is genre specific. Neither enrichment, nor our ideas of community, nor common knowledge, nor comparative advantage are restricted to some `high-brow' ghetto. What will matter most of the time is not *what kinds* of programmes are made, but *how* they are made – hardly the task for a regulator.

In addition, in the late 1990s there are two reasons why rules-based intervention will be less effective. First, there is technical change. At the moment the Government retains the ability to allocate frequencies and so regulation can be enforced. However, as satellite broadcasting becomes more widespread such regulation becomes more difficult. For example, within Europe there will be a number of satellite broadcasters each of which is aiming primarily at a single country, but whose signal can be received in a number of surrounding countries. If so, which countries' regulations apply? And how is the 'external' broadcaster to be forced to comply with two sets of possibly incompatible regulations? The answer to such problems is not to conclude that regulation is impossible, but to reconsider the objectives and to see whether there is some other way of influencing the market. One obvious possibility is to use public service broadcasting.

Second, there is the new commercial climate. The ITV companies are now traded on the stock exchange. They are also operating under the new franchise system and are under greater threat from cable and satellite. These developments have increased the pressure to maximise profits and, frequently, short run profits at that. This is a marked change from the position in the 1960s and 1970s when the system had a degree of slack in it which allowed the private companies to strike a balance between, on the one hand, their commercial concerns and, on the other hand, the public service obligations placed upon them by the legislation. In short, any purely regulatory system will be operating under far more strain than in the past. The alternative way of influencing the market, via the presence of public service broadcasting, is therefore, again, more rather than less relevant.

However, if such a public service broadcaster is to exist there has to be some stability of the institutional framework in order to maintain and extend standards and practices. Professional behaviour, a culture of quality and a commitment to the ideals of public service broadcasting do not exist *in vacuo*. They require an institutional context to sustain them.

The inescapable conclusion of all these arguments is that there should be a `centre of excellence', such as the BBC, which both makes and broadcasts programmes. It is possible that there could be more than one such centre (as it could be argued there is now with the BBC and, though in a different way, Channel 4), but the need for a critical mass suggests that at most there would be two or three such institutions rather than a series of independent producers.

One final point remains to be made. Almost all discussion of public service broadcasting on the one hand and the market on the other founders on a major misunderstanding about choice. In the minds of the critics of the BBC it is clear that the fear of censorship and, in particular, of hidden censorship has loomed large. Such fears and criticisms were understandable in the past when spectrum scarcity prevailed and when, as a result, access to televisual media was, as the critics would have said, exclusively under the control of either state funded or state authorised institutions. But this will not be the broadcasting world of the next century. Satellite, cable and video mean that private televisual media will expand considerably irrespective of the role played by public broadcasters. As a result, in this new world, provided only that the costs are met and the general law of the land is respected, no one will be *denied* making or seeing anything they wish.

On the contrary in the face of the new technology which threatens excessive fragmentation, the loss of common knowledge and low quality, it will be the existence of a public service broadcaster which *widens choice* and which, through its commitment to provide understanding, gives the *means to make the choice for oneself.* Thus a vibrant commercial system *plus* a context influenced by public service broadcasting would be the very opposite of elitism, paternalism or censorship.

In other words, public broadcasting is needed for the health of the *whole* system. Thus the BBC, or something very like it, is central, not an optional add-on. In short, such a public service broadcaster is a real public good and the true justification for public funding is not the 'financing the BBC', but the financing of the quality of the system.

Just as in the nineteenth century no one thought that regulation could *provide* public libraries so in the twenty first century regulation cannot provide public service broadcasting. Public service broadcasting exists to meet goals that are *not* those of the market and no amount of regulation can make the market pursue such goals. Thus while the BBC has no *right* to exist, there are *purposes for its existence*.

9 The Implications for Public Finance

If public service broadcasting is required, how is it to be financed? Should the funding take the form of a direct grant from Government and thus be part of the annual programme of public expenditure or, as now, be provided through a licence fee or a hypothecated tax? And, in either case, should the public funding provide the whole revenue or should some come from the private sector? If a special tax were appropriate, what form should it take and how large should it be?

9.1 Direct grant or special tax?

Three considerations suggest that public funding should *not* take the form of a direct grant from Government and thus be part of the annual programme of public expenditure.

First, there is the need for the institution to be seen to be, and to believe itself to be, at arm's length from the Government. This is a prerequisite for it sustaining a reputation for impartiality and for fearless reporting. Its independence from Government is just as important as its freedom from immediate commercial pressures. It is notable that Australia (relying on grants) is a country where the scale of funding has been increased or decreased – in recent years, mostly decreased – for political purposes.[20] Furthermore, there would be an ever present likelihood that the grant for the BBC would be squeezed in order to create room for extra spending in areas which were particularly pressing politically at the time.

Second, it is essential for any broadcaster's ability to maintain and extend quality that it be able to take a medium view of its future plans. Direct annual funding would not permit this.

Third, it is only with secure funding over a run of years that a public service broadcaster will be able to avoid the opposite temptation of boosting its income from commercial sources and then finding itself, as a result, being faced with a confusion of purpose.

The last of these considerations is highly pertinent to the merits, or otherwise, of 'mixed' public and private systems of finance. An organisation such as the BBC can either be asked to maximise its profits or it can be asked to maximise the effectiveness of its public service broadcasting. It *cannot*, however, sensibly be asked to serve two masters, attempting to maximise both simultaneously. Moreover, in the future the whole of broadcasting will be more de-regulated. As a result the commercial pressures both *on* the rest of the industry and *from* the rest of the industry will be higher than in the past. In the new environment there will therefore be an *increased* need for the BBC to concentrate on its public service role and for it to be neither pulled by commercial considerations nor pushed by short-term pressures of a different kind from government. These arguments suggest that it would be as much a mistake to go for 'mixed' public and private finance as to go for a direct government grant.

Advertising would also not be a suitable form of finance.[21] Once the BBC ventures down this path, it will almost certainly be forced to proceed further, until eventually it becomes indistinguishable from a commercial broadcaster. Indeed, any form of commercial finance, if it becomes too large, should be viewed with suspicion. This includes the development of income from 'sponsorship', which may at first seem attractive, but in fact simply represents advertising in a more insidious form. So, if the UK is to have a successful public service broadcaster, we simply have to resort eventually to some form of general funding.

Ideally, such general funding should fulfil the following characteristics. First, consumers should be able make a direct link between the benefits they receive, and the outlays they make. This suggests a flat rate charge (with the same charge made on everyone). Second, there should be some form of income-elasticity so that receipts from the charge grow faster than nominal GDP (essential for public service broadcasting to share in the general growth of an expanding economy). Third, the setting of the charge should be subject to minimum interference from the government of the day and fourth, the charge should be relatively easy to collect, enforce and administer.

Although the licence fee has been widely criticised in the past, it remains an efficient and cheap-to-collect form of taxation. The one major problem with the licence fee is that it has lost its buoyancy. Licence fee income grew quite rapidly both in real and nominal terms up to 1985, but has risen hardly at all since then. This slow down was the conjunction of two effects. Until the mid 1980s the number of households with colour televisions was growing rapidly, but by 1985, when the proportion had reached 86 per cent, this natural buoyancy was coming to an end. Then, from 1986 onwards, the Government pegged the increase in the licence fee to the Retail Price Index (the RPI). As a consequence from 1970 to 1985 real licence fee revenues rose by 4.4 per cent per annum, but from 1985 to 1996, real revenues rose by only 1.5 per cent per annum.

A major further problem for the BBC is that the BBC's costs (overwhelmingly labour costs) are likely to rise more rapidly over the medium term than the RPI. In the last few years the BBC has been able to overcome this problem by rapid increases in productivity, but this is almost certainly because there was a degree of slack in the organisation. Once this has gone the long run problem will reappear. It is difficult to tell how large this problem is as there is no official index of unit labour costs in the service sector. Nevertheless it is possible to derive such an index from the published numbers on services output, average earnings and employment. The resulting index shows an annual average rate of increase of 5 per cent per annum in the decade up to 1996. This is 0.5 per cent per annum faster than the increase in the RPI. In other words, if BBC costs grow at the same rate as those in the rest of the service sector, then it needs an increase in income of the RPI plus 0.5 per cent just to stay at its same size.

9.2 Possibilities for the future

These figures have important implications for the future. The automatic buoyancy that came from the move to colour television is over, yet the BBC needs an income that takes account of two characteristics. First, it must, as a minimum, rise in line with BBC costs (which, as shown above, rise faster than inflation). It is does not have this then BBC will gradually shrink in real terms. Second, it is to play the quality setting role which we have argued is so important, it must maintain its *share* of the market in broadcasting services. Over the next decade these are expected to rise rapidly. If the BBC's influence on the market is to continue, it follows that the real scale of the BBC must also rise – and so, therefore, must its income.

There are three ways in which this might be done. First, there could be a higher licence fee for digital televisions – just as there was for colour. If digital television were to spread widely, it could solve the BBC's problem of revenue buoyancy for many years ahead. The licence fee could be up-rated in line with the RPI or some other index, and the real growth in the service would be dependent on how rapidly digital TV sets penetrated the population. This approach has the added attraction that the spread of digital TV sets will probably be reasonable indicator of what will be happening to broadcasting services.

There are, however, objections to this proposal. No one knows how rapidly digital television will spread so there will be uncertainty and a higher licence fee for digital sets would be unpopular. In addition, at some point, analogue sets will be switched off. This will be unpopular whenever it happens, but all the more so if people are thereby forced to pay a higher licence fee. Moreover, once analogue is switched off, scarce spectrum will be released; the sale of which might bring substantial revenue to the Government. A disincentive to switch to digital might therefore be regarded as undesirable in policy terms. Nevertheless, higher charges for colour were widely accepted by the population, and created crucial buoyancy for BBC income.

Second, there could be a 'site' licence. This would be charged wherever households owned more than one television. It would be similar to how computer software is sold now to companies and other large organisations. In return for paying a premium households would be able to operate as many televisions (or computers capable of receiving television) as they wished. The advantage of such a system would be twofold. First, at the same time as charging a site licence the fee for a single set could be reduced – thus reducing the cost of television to those unable to afford more than one set. Second, once the system had been introduced it would have the crucial characteristic of some income elasticity (as more households become owners of two or more sets, revenue would rise). It would also avoid the disadvantage of slowing down the switch to digital TV. On the other hand it might be administratively complicated. In particular checking on the number of sets might require looking in people's homes. This alone might make it very unpopular, as would the higher payment for those owning more than one television. Moreover there is no neat correlation between ownership and income so some of the households who would be forced either to reduce the number of their TVs or to pay a site licence would include some poor households who could ill afford this.

Despite the objections, both of these options should be seriously explored.

The third possibility is that the licence fee should be increased more rapidly than inflation. One minimal move in this direction would be to up-rate the licence fee each year in line with unit labour costs in the service sector of the economy as a whole. On our data this would imply that the licence fee should be up-rated by 0.5 per cent per annum faster than the RPI. However, all this would do would be to stabilise the real level of BBC services that could be financed from the licence fee. There would be no scope for real growth, either in line with the growth in the economy, or with the growth in private broadcasting activity, which could be considerably faster. Consequently, the share of the BBC in the broadcasting market would still decline rapidly, unless alternative sources of revenue could be found.

To overcome this objection, the licence fee could be up-rated in line with the increase in overall labour costs, the 'wages bill' in the private service sector, rather than the increase in unit labour costs. The result would be an annual increase in the licence fee substantially above the rate of retail price inflation (probably by nearly 4 per cent per annum).

The objections are obvious. Consumers would not welcome regular increases in the real level of the licence fee and its regressive aspects would become more noticeable. However, the government used to include the TV licence in Supplementary Benefit payments and a similar system could be instituted in future. As far as consumers more generally are concerned the critical issues would be whether the case for such increases had been clearly made and how far consumers felt that the extra entertainment and information services were worth it. A closely related issue will be the level of prices charged by private broadcasters and the rate at which these will be increasing. Since the current charges for satellite or cable services are well above the licence fee, there may be more headroom than at first it seems. In any event if society wants the services which only a public service broadcaster can provide the costs have to be met somehow.

10 Summary and Conclusions

Who needs public service broadcasting? The answer is that we all do and that the new technology *increases*, not *decreases*, this need. The reasons are, first, that there is a real danger that if broadcasting were left just to the market it would become excessively concentrated; second, that even if this were not the case, commercial broadcasting on its own would fail to produce the form of broadcasting which people individually or citizens and voters collectively require; and, third, that there is no set of rules or regulations or laws which could entirely correct the deficiencies of a commercial system. This is for the simple but powerful reason that rules are necessarily negative. They have the capacity only to stop the undesirable. They cannot promote the desirable.

The only way to counteract fully the deficiencies of a purely commercial system is through the existence of a broadcaster, which has as its driving force the ethos of public service broadcasting.

Such a public service broadcaster would fulfil three crucial and inter-related roles. First, it would act as a counterweight to possible monopolisation of ownership and yet fragmentation of audiences in the private sector. Second, because its *purposes* were different, it would *widen* the choice that consumers individually and collectively would face. Third, provided it were large enough, it would have a positive influence on the quality and behaviour of the whole system. In brief, such a public service broadcaster is not an optional add-on, but central to the health of all broadcasting. The BBC does not have a *right* to exist, but it does have *purposes for its existence*.

As far as the source of finance is concerned, there is nothing better than the continuation of the licence fee. However, it should *not* be directly related to the RPI as at present. Broadcasting costs will grow faster than retail price inflation and, even over a relatively short period, will squeeze the BBC too much for it to be able to play the 'quality setting' role that is required.

The only way to guarantee such 'quality setting' is from an increase in the real revenue of the BBC. Extra revenue should come either from a higher licence for digital TVs, from a 'site' licence, or from increases in the licence fee well above the RPI.

One final point remains to be made. The BBC exists, does its job to international acclaim, and is, in general, highly appreciated at home. It would seem crazy, even just on insurance grounds, to start running it down *before* the effects of the new technologies and the de-regulation have come into anything like their full effect. If the BBC did not exist, it ought to be created with the utmost urgency. But endless experience demonstrates that the process of creation and destruction are *not* symmetrical. It would take a very brave or dogmatic policy-maker to be entirely sure that the arguments presented here will turn out to be wrong, and that the BBC will not be needed in the new environment. But once the BBC is destroyed, or fatally weakened, there may be no going back. It would be very difficult to re-create 75 years of public broadcasting culture once it had disappeared.

References

Bertelsmann Foundation (1995) *Television Requires Responsibility* Bertelsmann Foundation Publishers.

Forbes, J. (1989) 'France: Modernisation Across the Spectrum' in G. Nowell-Smith (ed) *The European Experience* British Film Institute, London.

Gallucci, C. (1994) 'How many votes did TV change?' *L'Espresso* 11 November.

Harding, R. (1985) 'Australia: Broadcasting in the Political Battle' in R. Kuhn (ed) *The Politics of Broadcasting* Croom Helm, London.

Lange, B-P. and R. Woldt (1995) in Bertelsmann *Television Requires Responsibility.*

Madge, T. (1989) *Beyond the BBC: Broadcasters and the Public in the 1980s* Macmillan, London.

Mepham, J. (1989) 'The Ethics of Quality in Television' in G. Mulgan (ed) *The Question of Quality* British Film Institute, London.

Noam, E.M. (1995) 'The United States of America' in Bertelsmann *Television Requires Responsibility.*

Peacock Committee (1986) *Report of the Committee on Financing the BBC* Cmnd. 9824. London, HMSO.

Williams, R. (1996) *Normal Service Won't Be Resumed: The Future of Public Broadcasting* Allen & Unwin, Australia.

Notes

1   This is a shortened and revised version of *Broadcasting Society and Policy in the Multimedia Age* by Andrew Graham and Gavyn Davies (John Libbey Media, 1997). I am grateful to John Libbey Media and Gavyn for the agreement to republish here in this form. The acknowledgements and thanks made there apply equally here.

2   Peacock Committee para 477.

3   Voice of the Listener and Viewer, 1996.

4   Proctor and Gamble had an earlier small interest in sponsoring broadcasting – hence the term 'soap operas'.

5   The initial researchers were working on projects for the US Department of Defence, who also provided the early funding, but the bulk of the research was in Universities or by people seconded from Universities.

6   It should be noted that the usual economic argument for charging for something (whether this is a 'price' or a 'subscription') does *not* apply to broadcasting because there is no question of anything being *scarce*. Broadcasts are a public good because one person's consumption does not compete with another person's consumption. It would therefore be perverse to insist that broadcasts become 'narrow-casts'.

7   Mepham, (1989) p.67.

8   It should be noted that we distinguish 'quality', which, by definition, cannot be measured, from 'standards', which might be measurable.

9   *Financial Times* 27 December, 1991.

10   Noam (1995).

11   Noam (1995) p.408 and 409.

12   Lange and Woldt (1995) p.484.

13   Madge (1989) p.59.

14   I owe this felicitous concept to Danny Quah.

15   Bertelsmann (1995) p.463.

16   Bertelsmann (1995) p.6.

17   President Clinton at the National Press Club, 11 March 1997

18   In economics 'common knowledge' is a technical term in the theory of games meaning what is known by all and is true. We use it here to cover a broader category of cases.

19   Quoted in Williams (1996).

20   See Harding (1985).

21   One of the great and lasting benefits of the Peacock Report was that it showed the advertising route for BBC finance to be a treacherous cul-de-sac.

Chapter 2

The Implications of Funding for Broadcasting Output

Christian Koboldt, Sarah Hogg and Bill Robinson

1 Introduction

Technological developments have fundamentally changed the nature of broadcasting. Where there used to be a limited number of terrestrial channels, satellite and cable television have brought about an increase in transmission capacity and a proliferation of channels. Sophisticated conditional access systems allow broadcasters to offer their services on a subscription or pay-per-view basis. Digitisation further increases channel capacity, and opens up the potential for qualitative as well as quantitative change. A blend of traditional broadcasting services with elements of interactivity and network intelligence may create services that are quite distinct from what traditionally has been perceived as broadcasting.

This proliferation of channels, services and ways of paying for the services can be expected to pose challenges for public service broadcasters. The BBC, traditionally funded from a licence fee levied upon every household owning a television set, has faced increasing competition from broadcasters that rely on more market-based mechanisms for their funding.

With the removal of capacity constraints on delivery, it has been argued that broadcasting could and should become more market-based. In general, after all, market outcomes are supposed to reflect consumer choice most closely. With this in mind the previous government committed to a review of licence fee funding before the mid-point of the BBC's Charter. The Labour government is now embarking on that review.

A central issue concerns the extent to which in a multi-channel, multi-broadcaster world, public service broadcasting should be funded mainly or exclusively through a licence-fee. In the mid-1980s the Peacock Commission proposed subscription as an alternative to the licence fee. The current review is asked 'against the expectation that the licence fee will remain the principal source of funding for public services for the Charter period [to]:

- consider ways in which funding to support public service output can be extended from other sources; and

- take a forward look at other possible mechanisms for funding the BBC in the longer term ...'

However, public service broadcasters, have repeatedly argued that a change in the way in which their services are funded would inevitably result in a change in output. Thus, even if broadcasters such as the BBC could survive as commercial organisations, they would be forced to change their behaviour in a way that would erode their role and conflict with their public service remit. Hence, it is argued, such a change would be undesirable from a social point of view.

In this paper, we examine the theoretical relationship between sources of funding and the nature of broadcasting output, in order to cast light on the core question: how could the erosion of the licence fee system be expected to change the behaviour of the BBC?

Of course, in practice this relationship may not be as strong and as clear as would appear from a theoretical framework. The nature of broadcasting output is determined by both the incentives that arise from a broadcaster's funding mechanism, and any obligations it might have under its licence. Put differently, the presence of licence obligations may weaken, but not eliminate the link between funding and the nature of output. Within the constraints created by a broadcaster's licence, it will respond as much as possible to the incentives created by the funding mechanism.

We begin by briefly analysing the different funding mechanisms that are actually or potentially available to broadcasters and spelling out their well-known implications for the incentives faced by broadcasters deciding about the choice of programming. We then proceed to establish a set of criteria for evaluating output, in order to identify the differences that one would expect to result from a particular way of funding.

2 Funding Mechanisms for Broadcasting Services

In this section we provide a brief description of the different mechanisms that can be employed for funding the provision of broadcasting services. We draw a broad distinction between commercial funding, which relies entirely on voluntary payments made in exchange for a product or service, and public funding, where direct or indirect payment is to some degree enforced by the state. This element of compulsion inherent in public funding implies that the payments received by the broadcaster are not solely dependent on the individual choices made by its customers; rather, a public body ultimately responsible to the electorate determines the level of funding.

The distinction between commercial and public *funding* must not be confused with that between commercial and public service *objectives*. There is by no means a one-to-one correspondence between them. Public service broadcasters study the ratings as assiduously as commercial broadcasters. And although commercial funding forces broadcasters to take account of the needs of the markets they serve, it does not prevent them from taking account of public policy objectives as well.

That is why, in the past, the government was able to achieve certain public service objectives not only through public funding, but also without paying for them – by imposing licence conditions on broadcasters financed from commercial revenues. So long as capacity was scarce and licences highly valuable, this was a powerful tool of policy. Commercially-funded broadcasters had, in effect, two 'clients'. To secure the renewal of their licences, they had to meet programming obligations; to secure revenue, they had to sell programmes to viewers, or viewers to advertisers.

However the 1990 Broadcasting Act marked a decisive shift in policy towards the commercial broadcasters. Even though there are still positive programming requirements, there was a shift in focus from 'positive regulation' designed to achieve public service objectives, to 'negative regulation' designed simply to ensure that minimum standards of taste and decency were met.

Some public service obligations are still enforced on commercial terrestrial television in the UK, where the limited number of channels still attract the vast majority of viewers. Public service broadcasting is wholly or partly advertising funded in many countries (including, in the case of Channel 4, in Britain). But the proliferation of channels is steadily reducing both the power of the regulatory tool and perhaps also the perceived need to use it. When broadcasters had to pass through a narrow gate, the gate keepers could exact a toll in the form of imposing public service obligations. But now the technology allows newcomers to by-pass the gate, it is not easy to enforce those obligations, since it handicaps the incumbents in their competitive battle with the new entrants.

As long as it was possible to impose, monitor and enforce a public service obligation even on commercial broadcasters, the whole sector was strongly tilted towards public service. However, the less effectively a public service obligation can be enforced the more important the incentives and pressure created by the funding mechanism will become.

For the purposes of this analysis we look at the 'pure' incentives that result from a particular funding mechanism. Therefore, we treat for example advertising-funded broadcasting as a purely commercial activity. This should by no means be interpreted as a judgement on the way in which existing advertising-funded free-to-air channels in the UK discharge their current public service obligations; nor should it be seen as a statement about the behaviour of public service broadcasters who rely on both licence fee income and advertising revenues (such as, for example, the German broadcasters ARD and ZDF).

2.1 Commercial funding

Pay TV

Pay-per-view

Pay-per-view channels, where people pay a specific charge to watch individual special events such as sports matches or concerts, have been available in the US for about a decade and are becoming available in many European countries. In a pay-per-view system, viewers only pay for those programmes, such as a feature film or television coverage of a sporting event, that they choose to watch. Consequently, watching a particular programme has an explicit price attached to it. Pay-per-view is the only funding mechanism that perfectly matches an ideal price mechanism, in that consumers pay for exactly those goods and services they choose to consume. They are able to signal clearly how much they are willing to pay for particular programmes, and prices – and hence supply – will reflect this. The success of pay-per-view may depend on the viewers knowing in advance more or less what they will get for their money and hence how much they are prepared to pay for it. This tends to be true of recent feature films (because they are heavily promoted) and of sporting events (because fans are well informed and because the big events are part of a recurring series of similar events).

Subscription charges

Subscription charges are collected for bundles of programmes (eg channels or bouquets of channels). Subscribers acquire the right to watch any programme in the bundle, at no extra charge. While pay-per-view is like downloading an individual news story from a paid-for on-line service, taking out a subscription is more like buying a newspaper. Basic channels are usually offered in large packages, through which premium channels can be bought. Channel bundling, including the choice of channels to be offered as separately paid-for premium channels, is one of the most important strategic decisions made by subscription broadcasters. Subscription bundles are designed to meet particular and known interests of target subscribers as surely as the *Sun* or *Daily Telegraph* do.

Secondary exploitation of programme rights

Secondary exploitation takes two forms: the re-selling of programmes (and/or video) by the broadcaster itself, and the sale of TV programmes to other broadcasters, either domestically or internationally. Digital television, leading to increasing capacity and an increasing number of channels, provides extra opportunities for the repackaging of programming originated by a particular broadcaster. This increases overall demand for broadcasting material, and thus the opportunities for sales to other broadcasters. However, it also extends the scope for secondary use by a broadcaster of its own material. The traditional form of such secondary use – repeats – can be replaced by re-using own material in order to provide value added services such as catch-up TV or genre channels which might be offered, for example, in a subscription window.

Regardless of whether programme rights are sold to rights buyers, or broadcasters decide to exploit an existing stock of programming themselves through the provision of value added services, this form of generating income is available only to broadcasters that produce their own original programming (whether in-house or through commissions), and is limited in scope by the extent to which they can do so.

Programme sponsorship

Where a sponsor pays the broadcaster for the right to be associated with a particular programme or type of programming, it is mainly the sponsor, not the viewer, who is the direct customer: viewers are the product that is being sold. However, it is rare for sponsorship to cover the full cost of the programming so the interests of the sponsor have to be balanced against the potentially conflicting interests of other providers of funding. This is a classic example of 'mixed funding'.

Although sponsors, like advertisers, may wish to reach certain types of audiences, they may also be trying to associate their brands with particular activities. Cadbury's sponsorship of *Coronation Street* associates chocolate with a regular, relaxing activity; Texaco's sponsorship of Formula One associates its petrol with high-performance engines, speed and excitement.

Businesses may wish to associate themselves with high-quality or high-brow programmes, even if the audience is limited. In the US, the smaller upmarket audiences delivered by some networks have enabled them to obtain sponsorship from what are deemed to be 'top quality' corporations. The high prices obtained from sponsors have been sustained through a process of careful sponsor selection, and rationing of the number of programmes that can be sponsored.[1]

On the other hand, the interest of the sponsor in the perceived programme quality, and the implications of editorial context for the sponsor's brand image, may mean that sponsored programmes are regarded as having less 'integrity' Hence, programmes for which editorial independence is crucial (eg, news and current affairs, religious or political programmes) may be deemed unsuitable for sponsorship. By the same token it may be difficult to get sponsorship for drama that is too controversial or challenging.

Advertising

Funding through advertising has been the mainstay of many commercial channels and, to date, revenues have increased broadly in line with nominal GDP. Advertising-based broadcasting has some fairly obvious implications for programming policy. Advertising-funded broadcasters are in the business of selling audiences to advertisers rather than offering programmes to viewers, and are therefore mainly concerned with the size and demographics of the audience they attract. They need to attract very large audiences, or smaller, but well-targeted audiences of high value to advertisers (which implies both a high income and a high propensity to respond to particular advertisements).

Advertising-financed broadcasters therefore have an incentive to avoid making controversial programmes covering important but 'difficult' subjects (eg a documentary on Auschwitz). They are concerned with the value their viewers place upon the programmes only to the extent that this is reflected in higher advertising revenue. This means that a prime motive tends to be ensuring that there is nothing in the material that will make viewers switch off. So the kinds of programme that enthral some viewers but make a large number of others switch off or switch over, are not attractive to the advertising funded broadcaster.

2.2 Public funding

As noted above, the main characteristic of public funding is that viewers have little or no direct choice as to whether they pay for the broadcaster's services. Broadcasters' freedom to choose their output is constrained not by individual viewers' choices but by official guidelines as to the nature of their 'public service obligations'. The final constraint, however, is that there must continue to be sufficient public support for what is provided to give confidence that governments will wish to maintain public funding. This implies that the public must perceive the 'value for money' they perceive to get from publicly funded broadcasting services to be sufficient not to want governments to abandon this form of funding.

Licence fee funding

The licence fee has been the predominant source of BBC finance. On several occasions since its introduction, governments have seriously considered replacing it with alternative methods of funding such as a government grant out of general taxation. The licence fee system has, however survived all such challenges in the UK.

One important feature of licence fee funding is that it should in principle give the BBC an equal relationship with each licence payer. Everybody pays the same, so everybody's view has the same weight. Funding from general taxation is different because the better off contribute a much higher proportion of tax revenue. This would tend to give their views on the BBC greater weight. In practice, under both kinds of public funding there is a risk that, despite best efforts to avoid such an outcome, the views of vociferous minorities may attract more attention, and perhaps carry more weight, than those of the silent majority.

In the early days of television, when buying a TV set provided access only to programmes offered by the BBC, the licence fee was merely a subscription for its services. As other television services became available, however, it became clearer that the licence fee is more like a hypothecated tax on television ownership and use. Subscriptions are voluntary, taxes are compulsory, and the owner of a TV set has no option but to pay the BBC licence fee whether or not he or she watches the BBC. In this respect the television licence is quite unlike other subscriptions.

However, the licence fee continues to be an identifiable payment (or 'hypothecated tax') which finances a specific range of services. Viewers are therefore able to reach their own conclusions as to whether the licence fee represents 'value for money' and much of the BBC's own self-publicity aims to reinforce the perception that it does.

General grant aid

Where a broadcaster is funded out of general taxation, the links between payment and service are less clear. It is harder for viewers to form their own opinion as to whether they are receiving value for money, since their own specific contribution will not be known. Nor, of course, will individual contributions be the same, since the incidence of general taxation depends on variable factors such as personal income and expenditure.

A further distinction arises from the system for deciding elements of general public expenditure: while these are theoretically fixed on a medium-term basis, there is an inevitable risk of annual adjustments as government grapples with the pressure of priority demands for limited resources. This leads to greater insecurity of funding, compared with a licence fee. Certain arm's length arrangements (such as lottery funding) offer a greater degree of medium security; but these, too, are subject to the pressure of competing priorities.

In theory, a grant could be specified as a fixed share of the revenue from a particular tax, (eg VAT or income tax). In this case, funding would then possess a certain buoyancy, growing roughly in line with GDP. However, there are two obvious drawbacks with this approach: it does not provide a mechanism for dealing with unexpected movements in broadcasting costs, so quality could suffer if costs rose. And conversely if broadcasting costs fell, and/or other public spending needs rose, there would be strong political pressure to adjust the formula to divert resources from broadcasting to other needs.

There is a further clear consequence of absorbing broadcasting costs within general government income and expenditure: increasing pressure on the 'arm's length' independence of the broadcaster. The more secure and predictable the funding system, the less broadcasters are likely to bend to the political wind in the short term. Thus, a government that truly seeks to maintain broadcasting independence will need to maintain distinct funding arrangements, which could take the form of a specified formula for determining the size of the grant from which the government cannot deviate. However finding a formula which is as binding on governments and as raid-proof as the licence fee is, in practice, not an easy task.

3 Evaluating Outcomes

The brief description of various funding mechanisms in the preceding section has given some indication how funding, which in essence determines who the broadcasters' customers are, tends to affect the choice of programming, in terms of content, diversity, quality and scheduling. Although this link between the source of income and a broadcaster's incentives is crucial for the implications of funding for output, it does not allow us to evaluate the different outcomes in terms of the public policy criteria which underpin public service broadcasting.

In order to take this second step, we need to establish a set of criteria for evaluating the outcomes that result from a particular funding mechanism. These may be derived from explicit public policy objectives, such as those outlined in the formal agreement between the BBC and the Secretary for Culture, Media and Sport, which accompanies the BBC's Royal Charter and specifies service and standard obligations. Under this agreement, the BBC has committed itself to offering a wide range of high-standard programming, including programmes that stimulate and reflect the UK's diverse cultural activity, original programmes for children and young people, and a comprehensive, authoritative and impartial news coverage.

For the purpose of this analysis, however, we have returned to certain basic principles in order to construct our tests. These enable us to apply some fundamental economic analysis rather than rely entirely on qualitative and perhaps highly subjective assessment of the value of certain types of programming.

3.1 The concept of economic efficiency

Economists usually employ the criterion of 'economic efficiency' in order to evaluate outcomes. 'Economic efficiency' (sometimes also referred to as 'Pareto-optimality') refers to a situation in which no one could be made better off without making somebody else worse off. Efficiency, so defined, should be generally acceptable as a public policy objective – unless, of course, someone has a preference for making people miserable. The reason for this is simple: greater efficiency means that there is more for everyone.

In order to be efficient, an outcome has to meet a number of conditions.

- A particular good or service should be *produced* efficiently. This implies that a given quantity of a product of a given quality should be produced at the lowest possible cost.

- A good or service should be *used* efficiently. This implies that everyone whose valuation exceeds the cost of supplying it should end up consuming the good or using the service.

- All goods or services which customers value more than they cost to supply should be produced.

Competitive markets and efficiency

There is a general presumption that competitive markets lead to economically efficient outcomes. In such markets, the level of output and the price at which it is traded are set by equating supply and demand. This determines 'equilibrium'. Competition selects the suppliers who can produce the equilibrium quantity at the lowest cost; and ensures that the consumers who most value the good are the ones who actually purchase it. At the equilibrium price, there are no potential consumers who would be willing to pay more for the product than it would cost to produce additional units. Otherwise, there would be profitable opportunities for further production and trade that would make both producers and consumers better off.

The efficiency of market outcomes derives from the fact that prices signal to producers and consumers the value and cost of producing or consuming an additional unit of the good. In addition, the *social value* (ie, the value to society as a whole) of consuming an additional unit of the good at the equilibrium price is normally equal to the *individual value* (ie, the value to the individual who purchases the good), and the *social* and *individual* values of producing the good are also equal.

Public goods and market failure

However, the equality of individual and social values will not occur under all circumstances. Where social and individual values diverge, markets will usually not lead to efficient outcomes. This divergence occurs in, for example the case of what economists refer to as 'public goods'. Broadcasting is a prime text-book example of a public good.

Some goods and services can be 'consumed' by more than one person at a time without reducing the amount that is available to any other consumer. The pleasure I derive from looking at a great painting in a national gallery in no way reduces the pleasure available to the next art lover to view it. Broadcasting offers an even clearer example of this phenomenon. My decision to watch a television programme does not in any way prevent others from watching the same programme; we are not 'rivals' for its use. By contrast, consumption of certain other goods (ie food) is 'rivalrous': what is consumed by one individual cannot be consumed by another.

As Hirshleifer and Glazer [2] put it:

> ...a good is 'public' if providing the good to *anyone* makes it possible, without additional cost, to provide it to *everyone*. Note that the definition does not require that different people get the same enjoyment from the good; people can consume identical quantities without enjoying the same benefits from it.

This distinction between 'rivalrous' and 'non-rivalrous' goods has important implications for their valuation. The social value of the food we eat is limited to the individual value put on it by the one consumer who eats it. Competitive markets will ensure it goes to the consumer who places the highest value on it.

In the case of the 'non-rivalrous' goods, however the social value is given by the *sum* of everyone's willingness to pay. The social value of a TV programme is not represented by my individual valuation, but by the aggregate valuation of all those people who might watch the programme. There is no reason why consumption should be restricted to the person (or the group of persons) with the highest willingness to pay, because their 'consumption' does not reduce the amount of the good that is available for others. A market mechanism which excluded consumers who are not willing to pay a certain price would not, therefore, lead to an efficient outcome.

Social policy

The analysis of economic efficiency we have conducted so far does not, however, take account of some qualifications that need to be added to the assessment process. These concern social policy objectives, such as equity, or public service objectives, such as the provision of 'merit goods'.

Merit goods

The concept of economic efficiency is based on the principle of *consumer sovereignty*. Individuals are seen as the best judges of their own well-being, and their preferences are taken as given. Economic efficiency does not take into account the fact that some individuals may be foolish or myopic, and behave in a way that is not in their own best interest. This shortcoming has been addressed by introducing the concept of 'merit goods'. A merit good is one whose value exceeds the valuation an individual would place upon it. In other words, merit goods have an intrinsic value that is independent of the valuation given by individual consumers.

Clearly the concept of merit goods depends in practice on the presumption that someone knows what is in people's interest better than they do themselves. This smacks of an unacceptable paternalism which is at odds with the methodological underpinnings of economics. On the other hand there are value judgements that are widely shared within a society: the government provides access to health care, museums, libraries and opera either free or at prices well below cost. These are examples of merit goods where paternalism is underpinned by democratic consent. If that were not the case they would not have survived.

Recent work has attempted to reconcile the concept of merit goods with the principle of consumer sovereignty. Such work has rested on the empirically well-established fact that people's preferences are sometimes inconsistent, or in other words, that people may seem to be of two minds. For example, viewers might in general recognise that it would be in their interest to watch more informative or educational programmes; but after a long and tiring day, opt for light entertainment rather than QED. We will explore the implications of this interpretation of merit goods in our analysis below, while retaining a certain scepticism; such arguments move one from objective analysis to hypothetical arguments about viewers' states of mind, and need to be treated with caution.

Equity

The analysis of economic efficiency does not capture concerns about equity. As Professor Sen has put it:

> An economy can be optimal in this sense [of economic efficiency], even when some people are rolling in luxury and others are near starvation as long as the starvers cannot be made better off without cutting into the pleasure of the rich. ... In short, a society or an economy can be Pareto optimal and still be perfectly disgusting.[3]

In other words, although it is desirable to avoid economic inefficiency not all economically efficient outcomes are equally desirable. In analysing the sources of funding for broadcasting, therefore, it is important to take into account their sensitivity to public policy objectives with respect to equity.

Issues of equity may seem less important in an age when broadcasting capacity is no longer a scarce resource, and competing producers will offer a range of services to different viewers. Where broadcasters face no additional costs in supplying the marginal viewer, a range of different mechanisms will offer access to low-income groups. On the other hand viewers may well be denied access to programming where the fixed costs are high, and the broadcasters attempt to recoup those costs through a charging mechanism of some sort.

Stability of income

A number of cultural considerations have given rise to the view that stability of income is an important criterion for broadcasting funding. It is argued that the ability to experiment, to innovate, to diversify and satisfy minority interests is heavily dependent on certainty about future funding. It is also the case that good programmes such as major drama or documentary series can take a long time to produce. Taken to its extreme, of course, this argument can easily be challenged – it can equally be argued that it is the need to secure future income in a world of changing tastes and habits that forces broadcasters facing income insecurity to innovate and respond to viewers' demands. Nevertheless, for the purposes of this analysis we consider it important to categorise funding mechanisms according to the degree of stability of income that they provide, noting that stability can have both desirable and undesirable properties.

3.2 The basic trade-off

The public good characteristics of broadcasting have important implications for the provision of broadcasting services. Any funding mechanism that excludes some viewers whose valuation of the service would exceed the cost of supply necessarily leads to inefficiency and welfare losses. These welfare losses result from restricting the viewing of programmes that, once produced, could be made available to everyone at no extra cost. A system such as pay-per-view, where viewers pay a price for every programme they watch, will involve inefficiency to the extent that it results in such welfare loss. We call this the *welfare loss from exclusion*.

Such welfare losses can be avoided only if broadcasting services are supplied free at the point of use. However, broadcasters then need to rely on other sources of funding in order to cover their costs. These other funding mechanisms, in turn, may have characteristics which lead to a loss of economic efficiency. Most notably they may fail to reflect or respond to the valuation viewers individually place on the programmes they receive. This may lead to welfare losses, because programmes that are valued highly may not be provided by broadcasters; while less highly valued programmes may be produced. We call this the *welfare loss from absence of price signals.*

An example may help to clarify this important point. There may be a minority programme – live transmission of an opera first night at Covent Garden for example – that attracts a relatively small audience. But those who watch it value it enormously. Since demand for seats at the opera exceeds supply, even at a price of £100 per seat, opera buffs might be willing to pay (say) £5 per head for the televised version. Even if the audience were only a few hundred thousand, tiny in television terms, the revenues would be well in excess of costs. Under a pay-per-view system, the broadcaster would find the venture commercially worthwhile. So a transmission that is clearly in everyone's interest would take place.

If however there were no pay-per-view, and the broadcaster bases his decisions purely on ratings, the opera may very well not be transmitted. Since, in this example, the welfare gain of the opera buffs who would have watched it is well in excess of the costs of transmission, there is a welfare loss resulting from the absence of the price signal. Such welfare losses are endemic in the world of advertising funded broadcasting, where scheduling is driven by the numbers of viewers rather than by the amount they value the programmes on offer.

But this does not mean that pay-per-view solves all problems. To see this, let us consider a different example, a classic serial such as *Middlemarch*. Let us suppose that *Middlemarch* was enormously valued by a minority of George Eliot fans, to the point where, had the programme been on pay-per-view, they would have willingly paid £3 per episode. But suppose that the number of enthusiasts prepared to pay this price is again only a few hundred thousand, and that the revenue from pay-per-view at that price does not meet the production cost. Then we might conclude that the programme will not be made.

But let us take the argument a stage further, and consider all the people that watched and enjoyed *Middlemarch*. Some of them might have been prepared to pay £2, or £1 or 50 pence or 10 pence. The problem is that to capture the millions of viewers who would enjoy the programme at 10 pence, you have to charge 10 pence to everyone. And once again you find that the revenues are not sufficient to meet the production cost. A programme of this sort, with a few viewers who value it highly and a long tail of viewers who value it less, does not lend itself to pay-per-view because however you set the price the revenue is less than the cost of making it.

However, it is clear that there is a very large amount of revenue that a perfectly discriminating monopolist could extract from *Middlemarch* if he could charge each viewer exactly what he or she is prepared to pay. That is the essence of the public service case for making such a programme and meeting the cost out of the licence fee. The problem with a world in which *Middlemarch* is available only on pay-per-view at £3 is that millions of viewers are prevented by the high price from watching it. The sum total of the enjoyment of those excluded by the charge is the welfare loss from exclusion.

The key point to note here is that the extent to which a funding mechanism (such as pay-per-view) allows viewers to signal their valuation is closely related to the extent to which that funding mechanism leads to exclusion (because the profit-maximising price is too high for many would-be viewers). This relationship translates into a basic trade-off in terms of welfare and efficiency:

- funding mechanisms that allow viewers to signal their valuations tend to lead to welfare losses from exclusion; and
- funding mechanisms that ensure that broadcasting services are offered at marginal cost (ie do not exclude) lead to welfare losses through a blunting of viewer valuations.

This would seem to indicate that a mix of funding mechanisms will offer the richest range of broadcasting, allowing viewers to trade off the welfare loss from exclusion and the welfare loss from absence of price signals. The nature of this mix depends, of course, on the relative performance of each of the funding mechanisms in terms of efficiency and welfare, and the interaction between different types of funding. We address this issue next.

3.3 Quality, valuation, merit and public policy

The terms quality, value, merit and public service are heavily used in the assessment of programming. They are, however, used to express rather different ideas, which it may be helpful to distinguish at this point.

- *Quality programming* tends to be defined with reference to the way in which it is produced: whether it is well-researched, original, has artistic merit, high 'production values', aims to challenge the imagination and intelligence and so forth. Quality programming will tend to be expensive, but only relative to the particular genre – and it is clearly not the case that all expensive programming displays 'quality'. It is, by and large, broadcasters who debate and conclude issues of 'quality' and decide how much it is worth paying to achieve it.

- *Valued programming*, by contrast, is defined by viewers – the definition rests on their valuations of what they like, and how much they are prepared to pay for it. Social valuation is, as we have seen, the aggregate of individual valuations. Although there may be quite strong correlation between 'quality' and 'valuation' (with respect, for example, to drama with high production values) it is important not to confuse viewers' and broadcasters' opinions as to what constitutes good television.

- *Merit programming*, in the economist's sense of 'merit goods', clearly does not correspond exactly with either of the above categories. We have argued that the best interpretation of this concept is as a variation on value – the programming viewers like to know is available even if on particular occasions they decide to watch something of less 'merit'.

- *Public service programming* may be used to encompass all three categories, and more besides. The distinction again lies in the answer to the question: who defines it? Public service is defined by elected politicians and officials on behalf of viewers (or voters). Clearly, however, if they diverge too far from viewers' valuations, public service broadcasting will cease to command popular support.

In an ideal world, broadcasters should provide the programmes that are most highly valued (where the value may be attached to programmes because they are merit goods). This is different from maximising quality. Quality, as defined above, is determined by producers. Value is measured by consumers. In many cases quality creates value, but sometimes it does not. There may be merit good arguments for quality programming which is valued at less than its cost.

The validity of all these concepts ultimately rests on individual valuation of programming. For years broadcasters have measured this in a rather crude way by focusing on the number of viewers who watch particular programmes. But this measure is clearly imperfect because it fails to capture the intensity of enjoyment of each viewer. To do this we really need to find out how much each viewer would have paid to watch the programme. Pay-per-view delivers this, though for only a tiny fraction of television output. Moreover it does so very imperfectly, because it does not tell us how much the *excluded* viewers *would* have paid for the programme, and it does not tell us how much more the *actual* viewers *might* have paid for the programme. The revenue generated by a pay-per-view programme is thus only a fraction of its total value to actual and potential viewers, and for some types of programme rather a small fraction (as we shall show).

There are two further problems with using pay-per-view revenue as a measure of value: there is a difference, potentially important for some kinds of programmes, between *ex ante* and *ex post* valuation; and there is the problem that each of us may value the existence of programmes even if we do not watch them.

How much viewers will pay to watch a programme depends on their *ex ante* valuation – how much they expect to enjoy it. Arguably the true value of the programme should be measured by their *ex post* valuation – how much they did in fact enjoy it. For many kinds of programming the two are very close – viewers know what to expect when they turn to *Blind Date*, and that is what they get. But many high quality television programmes are not in that category. The really memorable drama and documentary series will have a much higher *ex post* valuation – we simply did not realise how much we would value *Civilisation*, *The World at War*, or *The Forsyte Saga* until we saw them.

The other problem, of existence value, can best be illustrated by an analogy taken from environmental policy. Many of us value the existence of sites of outstanding natural beauty, and hate the idea of their destruction, even if they are in remote locations that we may never visit. Empirical attempts have been made to put figures on these values (which can be surprisingly large if very large numbers of people are each prepared to pay a small amount to preserve something).

Certain television programmes have a rather similar status. The fact that you can be sure of turning on the television at nine o'clock or ten o'clock to be given an authoritative and impartial summary of the main events of the day is something people value even if they do not avail themselves of the facility on a daily basis. We all recognise that the underlying news gathering network is costly and that it provides a valuable service. When nothing much is happening we may not bother to tune in. But we nevertheless value the fact that *The Nine O'Clock News* is there when we need it.[4]

3.4 A classification of funding mechanisms

Each of the funding mechanisms described in section 2 has certain unique characteristics. We have now established a set of criteria that we can apply, in order to evaluate their outcomes. We can seek to distinguish between funding mechanisms on the following grounds:

- *The extent to which the mechanism allows viewers to signal their valuation of programming.* This sensitivity to customer choice depends on the extent to which payments are related to the type of service received and the quantity used. At one end of the spectrum, a pay-per-view system enables customers to pay only for the specific programme they choose to watch. At the other, the licence fee reflects individual valuation only to the extent that the system satisfies viewers as a whole sufficiently well to secure their support for the continuation of the licence fee (though broadcasters dependent on the licence fee maintain sophisticated systems for monitoring audience reactions and are very ratings-conscious). In between those two extremes, subscription fees allow viewers to value bundles of programmes, which is likely to be more direct than the signal available to viewers of programmes financed by advertising, where viewers' ability to signal their valuation is restricted to the binary choice of watching/not watching the programme. This is fed back through payments received from advertisers, which in turn reflect the audience size achieved by a particular programme. By contrast, the amount subscribers are willing to pay for a channel package should provide a better indication of the value they place on receiving those services. However the precision of the subscription price as a signal of value decreases with an increasing size of the channel package, and ratings (which are closely and continuously monitored) may provide a better indication for the value of individual programmes, reducing (or even eliminating) the difference between subscription and free-to-air broadcasting.

- *The extent to which the mechanism leads to exclusion of viewers.* Any system of charging for individual programmes involves excluding some viewers who are not willing, or not able, to pay the price. Once television programmes have been made and broadcast, there is no additional cost in 'supplying' them to the extra viewer. There is therefore, from the social welfare point of view, an inefficiency in any form of funding system which is 'exclusive'. Again, pay-per-view is at one end of the spectrum, with licence fee payments and advertising funding at the other end, although on this score their positions are reversed. Even the licence fee may, of course, exclude a small number of households, (although in reality some of these people watch illegally). While advertising imposes no direct obstacle in the form of a fee, it could be said to impose an indirect one – if we believe that it detracts from people's enjoyment. But these mechanisms are clearly less exclusive than pay-per-view. Subscription systems are located somewhere in between: individual programmes in the package are free at the point of viewing, but viewers are excluded from programmes in packages for which they do not pay.

- *The extent to which the funding mechanism will support the production of 'merit goods'.* The principal determinant of this outcome is, of course, the extent to which government is either willing or able to impose obligations on broadcasters to supply programming which represents viewers' 'ideal' preferences. Thus a licence fee system will score strongly, while pay-per-view, which responds only to what viewers actually watch, will score only weakly – as will advertising-based funding. However, subscription-based funding may be somewhere in between (I may subscribe for 'merit' programming I do not actually watch much), while sponsorship funding may also score more strongly (sponsors may wish to be associated with what viewers perceive to be quality programming – even though they might not actually watch such programmes – seeing it as brand-enhancing).

- *The extent to which social policy objectives are likely to be met.* This criterion clearly depends even more heavily on government's ability to specify its objectives to broadcasters. As capacity becomes less and less scarce, this ability to lay down obligations as a condition of a broadcasting licence has been steadily undermined. Thus the funding mechanism becomes a much more important tool, and licence fee funding (or other public support) stands out as the mechanism which most clearly meets this criterion. However, other free-to-air mechanisms, notably advertising-funded broadcasting, score highly in terms of access.

- *The extent to which the funding mechanism provides a stable and secure source of income.* Certainty of future funding is deemed to be a positive effect, in that it is not merely convenient for broadcasters but encourages them to experiment in new programming and to invest in new technologies, such as digital broadcasting. Here again the licence fee marks one end of the spectrum, with general grant aid and pay-per-view both displaying much greater volatility.

A classification of funding mechanisms according to these criteria is provided in Table 2.1. The key columns are the first and second. As this classification shows, there is a general trade-off between the extent to which funding allows viewers to signal their preferences, and the extent to which it leads to exclusion. The remaining columns are inevitably more judgmental. And it is important to repeat that the assessment of commercially funded television relates to purely commercial channels, not to those that are subject to a number of public service obligations as the condition of a licence.

4 The Implications of Funding for Outcomes

4.1 The objectives of broadcasters

Although commercial broadcasters may have a number of public policy objectives incorporated in their licences (as, for example, in the case of the ITV companies or Channel 4), their main objective tends to be the maximisation of profits. They may have responsibilities to shareholders which, together with the competitive constraints they may face in the market place, determine their choice of programming, attitude to costs and the prices at which they offer their services to viewers or advertisers.

Even where such broadcasters are subject to public service obligations through their licence, they can be expected to maximise profits *subject to the additional constraints* imposed upon them. It is also worth noting that these profits need not be taken in the form of dividends to shareholders. They may be dissipated to viewers in the form of more or better programming.

Table 2.1: Extent to which funding mechanisms meet objectives shown

	Allows viewers to signal preferences	Allows access to all viewers	Stability of income (medium-to long-term)	Fulfilment of social policy objectives	Production of merit goods
PPV	very strong	nil	weak	weak	weak
Subscription	moderate / moderate (depending on size of package)	weak	moderate	weak	weak
Rights sales	strong	strong	moderate	weak	moderate
Sponsorship	weak	very strong	weak	weak	moderate
Advertising	moderate	very strong	moderate	moderate	weak
Licence fee	moderate	strong	strong	very strong	very strong
Grant-in-aid	nil	strong	weak	very strong	very strong

● = very strong ◕ = strong ◑ = moderate ◔ = weak ○ = nil

By contrast, the profit maximisation objective is muted in the case of publicly funded broadcasters who are instead governed by a set of public policy objectives that are often more wide-ranging than the objectives attached to commercial licences. However, even a partial dependence on commercial sources of incomes tends to introduce the same pressures and incentives faced by fully commercial broadcasters. If, for example, the BBC were mainly licence fee funded, but partly dependent on advertising revenue, it would for this part of its income be subject to the same incentive to maximise revenues (ie, the same pressure to compete for it) as a broadcaster funded entirely by advertising. Of course, the impact of such a change in incentives may be limited if advertising is limited to specific services or times (as, for example, in the case of Germany), but even then there may be some spill-over effects if broadcasters have an incentive to create an overall perception of their channel that maximises their audiences during the times when they are allowed to advertise.

4.2 Illustrative valuations

We can illustrate the issues discussed above and in the preceding section with some stylised examples based on a simple world where there are 14 (million) potential viewers, and four different kinds of programme. Each viewer places a certain valuation, or willingness to pay, on each of the four programmes. We measure these valuations by some illustrative (arbitrary) numbers. To keep the example simple we deal in units of a million viewers, each of whom is assumed to attach the same value to the programme. We order these units of a million viewers according to their willingness to pay, which gives us what are in effect demand curves for each programme, as shown in figure 2.1.

The diagrams illustrate four different *shapes* of demand curve, which as we show below will result in very different programming choices under different funding mechanisms. These different shapes are plausible descriptions of the following programme genres:

- *Small niche Programme A* has a demand function which could be characteristic of a specific sporting or cultural event (eg Rugby Union at club level or opera). There are a few viewers who value it extremely highly, while a lot of people would not choose to watch it even if it were offered free of charge.

- *Mass appeal, low value Programme B* attracts a wide audience but is not valued particularly highly by anyone. An example could be a game show or a sitcom.

- *Large special interest Programme C* could be a quality series (eg *Friends*) or a larger minority sports programme (snooker) valued positively by many people and highly by some of them. There are a few, however, who would turn the TV off when it is on.

- *Wide appeal high value Programme D* is a programme which attracts large numbers of viewers (though less than Programme B), some of whom value it extremely highly. A good example might be a news programme, one of the listed sporting events or perhaps a classic serial which wins large ratings (eg the legendary *Forsyte Saga*). The interesting characteristic of such programmes is that though they are *watched* by nearly everyone they are *valued* much more by some than by others ('everyone' watches the Cup Final but the true football fan could not bear to miss it).

On the supply side, we assume that there is a one-off fixed cost of making each programme and that all of them can be supplied to an additional viewer at no extra cost (in other words, the marginal cost of delivering the programme to a viewer is zero). We assume that if the programmes are funded commercially, the broadcaster chooses the price which maximises profits. We will show that programmes of one type rather than another will be systematically more attractive to the broadcaster, depending on the funding mechanism.

To understand this we need to distinguish six essential characteristics of the programmes, as shown in the demand curves:

- *The total value* created by transmitting each programme which is the area under the demand curve.

- *The profit-maximising price* for each programme if it were offered as pay-per-view or on subscription by a private profit-maximising supplier.

- *The revenues generated* by that programme at the profit maximising price, which is the rectangle in the middle of each demand curve. The size of these revenues measures the incentive to produce such a programme in a pay-per-view regime.

- *The consumer surplus* enjoyed by the viewers who might watch that programme under a pay-per-view regime – this is the difference between the price they would be asked to pay and the price they are prepared to pay. An individual who values a programme at £10 but has to pay only £5 enjoys a surplus of £5. The total of these surpluses is represented by the area under the demand curve, bounded below by the market price.

- *The welfare loss from exclusion* which results if instead of providing the programme freely at the point of use, the profit-maximising price is charged. This is the consumer surplus of those viewers who cannot afford to watch the programme at that price.

- *The number of viewers* which is where the demand curve meets the horizontal axis.

If we assume for the moment that all the programmes cost the same to produce (we consider the case of different programme costs below) then under different payment mechanisms, different programmes will be made:

- *The licence-fee funded broadcaster* would, if it had the information on valuations, make the programme which generates the most welfare.

Figure 2.1 Demand curves for different types of programmes

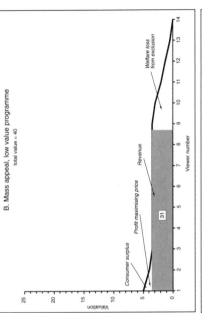

A. Small niche programme
total value = 57

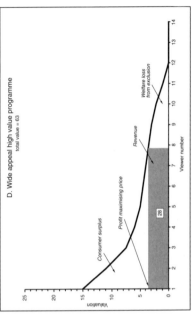

B. Mass appeal, low value programme
total value = 40

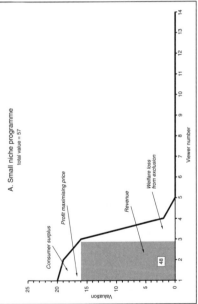

C. Large minority interest programme
total value = 75

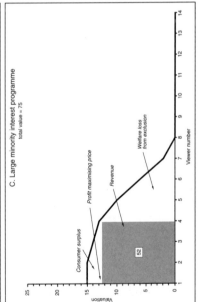

D. Wide appeal high value programme
total value = 63

- *The advertising funded broadcaster* will go for the programme which delivers the greatest number of viewers, irrespective of how much they value the programme.

- *The subscription or pay-per-view funded broadcaster* will go for the programme which delivers the most revenue and hence profits.

It is clear from this example that if the maximisation of social welfare is the objective, it could be met in an ideal world by securing the information on valuations and then putting broadcasting in the hands of a public service broadcaster with independent funding. In the real world there is a good case for using the information on valuations which comes from the market by allowing some pay-per-view or subscription-funded broadcasting. And there are also some kinds of programme which can perfectly well be funded by advertising. However there are problems with both these commercial funding mechanisms.

The problem with advertising funded programmes is well known. The incentive on the programme maker is to deliver the largest possible audience at lowest cost. The broadcaster does not ultimately care how much the viewers enjoy or value the programme. It is sufficient that they do not switch off. So advertising funding encourages the production of programmes with wide but shallow appeal. In a world where there was only advertising funding, Programme B (the game show or sitcom) would be shown in preference to Programme D (the *Forsyte Saga*), even though the latter creates more welfare.

Moreover, if there were only advertising funding, Programmes A and C, (club rugby matches and snooker tournaments) which are hugely enjoyed but by comparatively small audiences, might never have been shown. This would be a market failure, because as the examples show, they may actually create more social welfare than Programme B (the popular game show or the lottery draw), which is mildly enjoyed by large audiences. It might be thought that such a market failure would be corrected by the introduction of pay-per-view. We shall see that it is to some extent, but not entirely.

The small niche Programme A (club rugby matches) is an example of a genre which lends itself to pay-per-view. The key property illustrated by the diagram is that a high proportion of the value generated by such a programme can be captured by the broadcaster. The welfare loss from exclusion is relatively small, as is the consumer surplus of those who get the programme for less than they would be prepared to pay.

Programme D, by contrast, is an example of a genre which would not be made in a pure pay-per-view world. The *Middlemarch* example, discussed in section 3.2 above, showed how the commercial broadcaster seeking to make this kind of programme is in real difficulty. If he prices high to tap into the consumer surplus of the higher value customer, he loses a lot of revenue by excluding millions who would pay a moderate sum to watch the programme. But if he chases that end of the market by dropping the price, he forgoes an enormous amount of potential revenue from those prepared to pay the high price. The shape of the demand curve for this kind of programme is such that the revenue that can be extracted from the viewers is a small fraction of the total welfare. If the programme is expensive to make, it may not be made in a pay-per-view world, even if the total value of the programme is well in excess of the cost of making it.

Another kind of problem is illustrated by Programme C, which is the most attractive (because most profitable) proposition for a pay-per-view broadcaster. If a programme of this sort is only available on pay-per-view, there can be a large welfare loss from exclusion. This is because the profit-maximising price is high and even though relatively few viewers are excluded (compared with Programme D), many of them value it highly (imagine the uproar from addicts of *Friends* if it were restricted to pay TV).

In brief, in the advertising funded world, where the main driver is audience size, Programme B (the game show) will be made in preference to Programme D (the classic serial). In a pay-per-view world, where the main driver is profitability, Programme A (the opera) will be preferred to Programme D. Yet both A and B deliver less total value to viewers than D. Only public service broadcasters have the right incentives to make Programme D.

Table 2.2 underlines these points with some illustrative arithmetic. The first column shows the audience size. The second shows advertising revenues which we assume are based on numbers of viewers, at an illustrative rate of 3 per viewer. The third column shows the pay TV revenues based on the profit maximising behaviour illustrated in the diagrams. The fourth shows the value of each programme, which is the total area under the demand curve. The fifth shows the cost of making each programme.

Table 2.2 Programming incentives under different funding mechanisms								
						Would programme be encouraged by:		
	No of viewers	Advert. revenue	Pay TV revenue	Total value	Cost	Advert. Funding?	Pay TV?	Public service?
	(1)	(2)	(3)	(4)	(5)	(2) > (5)?	(3) > (5)?	(4) > (5)?
A. Small niche programme	4	12	48	57	30	No	Yes	Yes
B. Mass appeal, low value	13	39	31	40	30	Yes	Yes (just)	Yes
C. Large minority	7	21	52	75	50	No	Yes (just)	Yes
D. Wide appeal high value	11	33	28	63	50	No	No	Yes

We assume that the small niche programme and the mass-appeal low-value programme are both relatively cheap to make, at 30 units, whereas Programmes C and D are much more expensive at 50 units. We can then put ourselves in the shoes of an imaginary broadcaster and ask which programmes will be made under which funding systems. The answer, for the commercial broadcasters, is that the programme will be made if the revenues are greater than the costs. An examination of the figures in the table shows that:

- *The broadcaster dependent on advertising revenue* will, on these figures, find only Programme B clearly worth making. All the other programmes deliver audiences, and hence advertising revenues, which are too small.

- *The pay TV broadcaster* will certainly make Programme A, which is very profitable. He may just make Programmes B and C which are marginally profitable. He will not make Programme D which is very unprofitable.

- *The licence-fee funded broadcaster*, by contrast, will make all four programmes because for each of them the *value* exceeds the cost.

Table 2.3 below summarises these result. It shows very clearly how the funding mechanism results in a totally different order of preference for the four different kinds of programmes. The shaded area in the table indicates the programmes that will not be made under each funding mechanism on the assumptions spelled out above.

Table 2.3 Ranking of programmes made under different funding mechanisms			
	Advertising funded	Pay TV	Licence fee
1	B	C	C
2	D	A	D
3	A	B	A
4	C	D	B

5 Conclusions

There are many different possible funding mechanisms for broadcasting. None of them is ideal. Publicly funded broadcasting suffers from the defect that the link between payment (licence fee or taxes) and the programmes actually produced is not a close one. However closely public service broadcasters may monitor ratings, there are no *market disciplines* immediately to penalise them for producing radio and television that people do not value.

At first sight it might appear that this problem has now been solved. There have been advances in technology which have made it possible to distribute a wide variety of programmes down a large number of channels and charge for them. Thus it is now possible to create a proper market in television and radio programmes, just as there is a market in television sets or magazines.

However there is a fundamental problem in charging for any broadcast programme: the cost of serving the additional viewer is nil, and so any charge will exclude viewers whose enjoyment exceeds the cost of providing it. The arguments for having television free at the point of use are the same as the arguments for not imposing tolls on bridges and motorways: as long as there is no congestion there is a welfare loss from turning away the would-be user by charging him or her.

In a world in which one kind of funding mechanism (the licence fee) risks taking too little account of viewer choice while another (pay-per-view) can unnecessarily deprive viewers of the pleasure of watching programmes they had been used to receiving free of charge, there is much to be said for operating a mix of funding mechanisms. In other words there is a strong case for allowing broadcasters with different funding mechanisms to compete.

One of the ways in which we judge the success of funding mechanisms is by the variety of programmes that they generate. The case for public service broadcasting is that it provides funding for the production of programmes (that are valued by the viewers) that would not otherwise be made. This case is a very strong one when the only alternative is advertising revenues. What this paper has shown is that the case remains strong even when full account is taken of the new technology. There are still programmes whose full value to the viewers cannot be captured by the charging mechanisms currently on offer. There is still therefore a risk that in the absence of a licence-fee funded broadcaster such programmes would simply not be made.

Notes

1   Congdon *et al. Paying for Broadcasting – The Handbook*, Routledge, 1992.

2   Hirshleifer, J. and Glazer, A: *Price Theory and Applications*, 5th edition, Englewood Cliffs, 1992, p. 461.

3   Sen, A. *Collective Choice and Social Welfare*, Holden-Day, 1970, p. 22.

4   These examples illustrate some of the well-known arguments for public service broadcasting. Programmes are provided on the basis that they create additional social welfare that is greater than their cost. The social welfare is essentially the sum of individual valuations which cannot be revealed by the market but could in principle be assessed by questionnaires. Environmental policy is increasingly driven by valuations derived using these kinds of techniques.

Chapter 3

The BBC: Balancing Public and Commercial Purpose

David Currie and Martin Siner

1 Introduction

The BBC is one of the great success stories of British industrial performance. It is one of the very few British institutions that commands instant recognition and respect around the world. As a consequence, its international brand is one of the global leaders. It sustains its performance in production and broadcasting across a much wider range of genres than any other broadcasting group anywhere in the world. This has been achieved and sustained against the background of an industry subject to major technological change and a unique set of regulatory constraints: thus the BBC is constrained by its Charter in the way it spends its licence fee income; by the Foreign Office in the way it allocates the grant-in-aid for the World Service; and by competition policy in its commercial activities. Many organisations face some of these constraints and challenges; few face such a uniquely complex combination. The BBC's staying-power at the top of its business is a great British success, that is insufficiently recognised.

The key question for the BBC is how it will adapt and change in the face of the major technological changes – digital, the internet, the multiplicity of channels and broadcasters – that is now affecting the industry. How should it interpret its public service duties in this new age? What range of activities should it engage in, and what should be publicly funded from the licence fee and what should be run as a commercial operation. Above all, how far should the BBC's commercial activities extend, or should the BBC as a public service broadcaster hold its commercial activities in check?

The purpose of this paper is to consider the issues raised by the commercial activities of the BBC. The general case for public service broadcasting funded from the licence fee is made very effectively in the accompanying chapter by Andrew Graham, who argues that the need for this role is enhanced, not diminished, by the explosion of channels coming with the digital revolution. Without going over the same ground, we touch on some aspects of this in the following section of this paper. We then consider the general rationale for the commercial activities of the BBC, arguing that such activities are essential for delivering good value for the licence fee. We then examine the constraints placed on such commercial activities by public funding and general competition law. We then examine specifically the activities and performance of the two independently incorporated (though wholly owned) parts of the BBC: BBC Worldwide and BBC Resources. A final section draws together our main conclusions.

The basic case for the BBC's commercial activities is a no-brainer: the BBC as a publicly funded public service broadcaster produces a range of products that has value, probably increasing in the digital age, in the broader commercial marketplace, both at home and overseas. It makes good sense for the BBC to realise this value by sales, licensing and joint ventures, so as to increase the resources available to plough back into public service broadcasting. To refrain from that would be to weaken the BBC's ability to pursue its public service broadcast remit and to give poorer value for the licence fee. In the following sections we develop this argument.

If the answer to this high-level question is clear, there remain lower-level, but important, questions that also require answers. First, if it is desirable that the BBC engages in commercial activities, what is needed to ensure that these activities do not interfere with, or impede, its public service broadcast role? Second, if the BBC is to play both a public service broadcast role and a commercial role, what criteria determine which activities are to be publicly funded and what is to be commercial? Third, what constraints, if any, should be placed on these commercial activities? Finally, do the commercial and public service activities require different management structures and styles, and if so how should the BBC best organise these two parts of its activities?

2 The BBC's Role as a Public Service Broadcaster in the Digital Era

The aim of this paper is to examine the role and operation of the BBC's commercial activities. However, as the intention of these activities is *'to support public service broadcasting by maximising the benefit for the licence payer'*,[1] first we must provide the appropriate context by considering the BBC's public service role. To this end, we now outline the BBC's public service objectives and consider how they will be affected by digital technologies.

2.1 The rationale for public service broadcasting

The BBC's role as a public service broadcaster is governed by its Royal Charter (1996) and its Agreement (1996) with the Secretary of State for Culture, Media and Sports. The first objective of the BBC, contained in section 3(a) of the Charter, is:

> To provide, as public services, sound and television broadcasting services ... of information, education and entertainment for general reception ... in the UK (the Home Services) ... and for reception elsewhere ... (the World Service).

How is this general remit to inform, educate and entertain to be interpreted? It clearly includes the impartial news coverage (at home and abroad) for which the BBC is rightly renowned. It includes a commitment to educational programmes. It also involves a high quality of children's programming, which is crucial for the educational remit and which may well have lasting effects: exposing our young to television pap represents a poor investment in the future. More broadly, it also involves a commitment to the cultural life of the country, reflecting the lives and concerns of local and national audiences, marking events of national significance, reflecting and supporting the cultural diversity of multi-racial Britain, and covering sporting and leisure interests. This reflects the importance of sustaining and developing citizenship and community in British society, and supporting the flow of information and debate so crucial to democracy at home and abroad.

These requirements of the public services' programme content are spelt out in the Charter and the 1996 Agreement. They are supported by general commitments regarding programme standards, which include the provision of a balanced service, serving the tastes and needs of different audiences, to treat subjects with accuracy and impartiality and not to include anything which offends good taste or decency.

The need for a publicly funded public service broadcaster such as the BBC arises because market forces alone may well not meet these objectives.[2] This is because of the risk of market failure in the broadcasting market. This arises partly because of substantial economies of scale in production that may well generate an unduly concentrated industrial structure. It also arises because of externalities on the demand side which mean that the wish to see quality broadcasting that reflects broader values of citizenship and democracy may not be reflected in effective demand in the marketplace. The interaction of these supply side and demand side market failures makes the broadcasting sector especially vulnerable to the operation of pure market forces, with the danger of fragmentation and a decline of quality. The importance of broadcasting for the broader health of our society and democracy makes this an especially important area for public policy.

Given the need for policy intervention in broadcasting, a key question concerns its form. An important point is that the Charter affords the BBC considerable independence in fulfilling its public service broadcasting role, a sentiment echoed in the Agreement, subclause 2.1 of which states that the BBC:

> ... shall be independent in all matters concerning the content of its programmes and the times at which they are broadcast or transmitted and in the management of its affairs.

In effect, in its public service role, the BBC is given a broad mission to 'inform, educate and entertain', a mission that it has considerable latitude to interpret. This contrasts with the way in which independent television is regulated by the ITC through statutorily enforceable obligations regarding the amount and type of programming, not the general commitments laid on the BBC. The contrast is between the more negative, rule-based regulation ensuring appropriate standards in a commercial activity where profits represent the ultimate driver; and a publicly funded public service broadcaster whose primary purpose or mission is the pursuit of high quality broadcasting (subject to a funding constraint). There is a strong case for saying that the mission-oriented, public service broadcaster represents the more effective form of policy intervention, providing an important quality anchor to resist the downward quality pressure that market forces might otherwise exert if left to themselves.[3] We return later to the implications of this distinction for the BBC's commercial activities.

2.2 Public service broadcasting, the licence fee and the digital era

To fulfil the requirements of the public service role described above, the BBC is reliant on income from three sources: the licence fee, grant-in-aid and commercial activity. Although all these are important, and we will be discussing the latter at some length, the licence fee remains the most significant both in terms of the amount of income it provides (97 per cent of the Home Services total revenue in 1997/8) and in creating a rather unusual relationship between the BBC and licence fee payer – its viewers and listeners.

The structure of the broadcasting industry that has prevailed under analogue technology has a number of important characteristics that justify a licence fee funded, public service broadcaster. For example, broadcasting has the classic characteristics of a public good because one individual's viewing does not interfere with another's (although unlike some public goods, such as defence, an individual's consumption of broadcasting is optional). It is well established that left to market forces, the provision of public goods will typically be below the economically efficient and socially desirable level as a result of individuals attempting to free ride. Therefore, providing a free-to-air broadcasting service, funded through the licence fee, helps to remedy an important market failure. The case for free-to-air broadcasting is further supported, on the grounds of economic efficiency, by the high fixed costs, low marginal costs and scarcity of spectrum that prevail in the industry.

These arguments could also be applied to justify the case for an advertising funded channel, such as ITV, not simply a licence fee funded broadcaster. However, as we have already suggested, a commercially-driven broadcaster working within regulatory constraints is less likely to deliver effectively on the broader public service remit to 'inform, educate and entertain'. Even under present arrangements, ITV provides less coverage in some of the key 'public service' genres, particularly at peak times, such as factual programming, children's programming and current affairs.

For example, in 1997/8 BBC 1 broadcast an average of 5.1 hours of current affairs programming per week compared to 2.2 hours per week for ITV. With regard to news programming, BBC 1's schedule during peak hours contained over twice the amount of hours of the ITV. Similar patterns are observed across other genres. For example, BBC 1 and 2 together broadcast three times the hours of children's programming and documentaries and features than ITV.

If this is so when ITV is heavily influenced by the presence of the BBC, one may well ask what programming would result from sole reliance on a free-to-air advertising channel. Thus the experience of free-to-air broadcasting in the UK suggests that the 'heights' of public service programming are better met through a licence fee funded organisation than a commercially funded one.

Table 3.1 Comparison of ITV and BBC Schedules in 1997/8 (average hours/week)			
	BBC 1	BBC 2	All BBC	ITV
Arts & Music	2.1	5.0	7.1	5.8
Children's	14.3	14.9	29.2	12.1
Current Affairs	5.1	6.3	11.4	2.2
Documentaries & Features	23.8	66.7	90.5	30.5
Drama	17.5	8.4	25.9	26.9
Films	18.5	16.5	35.0	19.1
LE – Comedy	4.5	4.7	9.2	2.6
LE – Variety	9.4	7.0	16.4	11.1
National News	36.7	9.1	45.8	31.2
Regional News	3.5	0.1	3.6	5.7
Sport	11.9	18.2	30.2	7.6
All Factual	85.5	102.1	187.5	87.6

The digital era alters some of the arguments for the licence fee. Thus interactive services (such as On-Line and Video On Demand) have positive marginal costs, because additional usage increases the required capacity and bandwidth. This tilts the argument towards some other form of funding, possibly a volume charge, rather than relying solely on a fixed fee.

However, this does not mean that a licence fee funded, public service broadcaster will not play an important part in the future of the industry. This is recognised by the BBC's Royal Charter endorsed in May 1996, which allows for public service objectives to be met through analogue and/or digital means. Not only does this recognise the changes that are taking place in the broadcasting market but it also acknowledges the role that a public service broadcaster can play in it. One common objection to the extension of the public service role to digital is that for the near future this medium will be accessible only by a small minority of households, so that the near-universality of access implicit in the public service role is absent. But that is inevitable with a new technology: only a small minority had access to black-and-white TV and later colour TV in the early years of the launch of these technologies, and only later did penetration rise to cover almost all households. Yet few question that the BBC should have been at the forefront of the launch of these technologies. The same pattern must be expected with digital, and the same argument is valid for the BBC being at the forefront of this new medium.

The Charter granted to the BBC in 1996 not only supported its move into digital television and radio but also provided scope, subject to approval by the Secretary of State, for the development of commercial activities and international broadcasting. In endorsing these as core purposes of the BBC, the Charter was acknowledging the significant changes facing the BBC as a result of digital technologies. The nature of these changes and the rationale for the BBC operating commercial activities are discussed in section 3.

2.3 Conclusion

The important role played by the BBC in the political, cultural and social life of the UK is widely acknowledged. Funded principally through the licence fee, its Charter affords the BBC considerable freedom to meet its public service objectives of informing, educating and entertaining. As we enter the 'digital' era, these objectives remain very important, a fact recognised in the BBC's Charter which not only provides scope for the BBC to supply digital television and radio services but also endorses commercial activities as a core part of the BBC.

3 The Rationale for the BBC's Commercial Activities

The operation of commercial activities by the BBC is by no means new. As far back as 1923, when the *Radio Times* was launched, income from commercial sources has been used to support its public service programming. Many of the other commercial activities currently undertaken also began some time ago - in 1947, the Royal Wedding became the first BBC TV programme to be sold abroad and 1961 saw the publication of the Corporation's first book. However, as we discuss in subsequent sections, because of a variety of factors, the scope and importance of these activities has increased significantly in recent years. This process will continue following the granting of the Royal Charter in 1996, which effectively endorsed commercial activities and digital services as core objectives of the BBC. In light of the BBC's core public service objectives, it is important that a clear rationale for these commercial activities is established and, as significantly, that it is effectively communicated to the public. We now examine the rationale for these activities and the difficulties that the BBC may encounter in communicating it.

3.1 The rationale for commercial activities

The single most important rationale is that operating commercial activities helps to maximise the value of the licence fee to the benefit of viewers and listeners. Through paying their licence fee, these viewers and listeners have enabled the BBC to invest in and develop a variety of assets and intellectual properties, which are used in fulfilling its public service role - principally through free-to-air broadcasts. However, taking the case of a TV programme, it is possible for value to be extracted that goes beyond its initial free-to-air broadcasting. For example, in the case of the series *People's Century*, the rights have now been sold to broadcasters in over 40 countries. The income BBC Worldwide receives from these sales, as owner of the global rights, is then available to be reinvested in free-to-air programming.

In addition to selling programme rights internationally, further value can be realised from intellectual property domestically. This is achieved through offering convenient access to programmes, by selling videos, or by developing a programme brand across other media. The well-publicised *Teletubbies* provides a clear illustration of how income can be earned through these means. Although one might question the principle of selling a programme to individuals who have already paid for them (through the licence fee), it is important to realise that the products are different. A video offers not just access to a favourite programme but *convenient* access. In the case of other cross media products, such as books, magazines and CD-ROMs, these activities simply represent an extension of the principle established in 1923, with the launch of the *Radio Times*, which saw licence fee payers purchasing a commercial product made available by the BBC.

Failure of the BBC to take these opportunities to realise the full value of the licence fee on behalf of viewers and listeners could be viewed as an inefficient use of these funds. Maximising the return on the assets and intellectual property funded by the licence fee, subject to certain constraints, should be viewed as a key responsibility of the BBC in the same way that it is expected to operate as efficiently as possible. Naturally, if commercial income is earned then it should be retained within the BBC and reinvested in free-to-air, public service programming. Further constraints must also apply to these commercial operations. In particular, they should arise from public service programming and should not harm the BBC's brand; care must be taken to ensure they are not cross subsidised by the licence fee so that the BBC provides a source of unfair competition to the private sector, and that licence fee funds are not put at undue risk. These and other constraints are discussed further in Section 4.

Earning commercial income is not only important to realising the licence fee's full value, but also it is becoming an increasingly necessary source of finance for the BBC. This is due to two factors. First, because of political resistance to appreciable licence fee increases, the BBC's income from the licence fee has remained broadly static since the mid-1980s. Second, due to a combination of factors related to the increase in transmission methods available to broadcasters, the cost of securing access to talent and programme rights has been rising significantly.

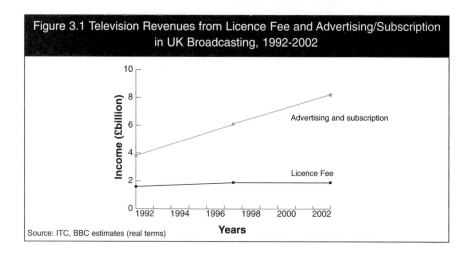

Figure 3.1 Television Revenues from Licence Fee and Advertising/Subscription in UK Broadcasting, 1992-2002

Source: ITC, BBC estimates (real terms)

The funding of the BBC via a licence fee was endorsed once again in the 1996 Charter. However, although the Charter has effect for 10 years, the status of the licence fee is only guaranteed until 2002 up to which time the BBC's income from this source will, in real terms, remain largely unchanged (see Figure 3.1). This is in contrast to the rest of the broadcasting market in the UK, which is funded through advertising and subscription. Although much of the income generated in this sector will be used to expand the number of channels (most of which will originate few programmes and those that do will be mainly be low budget productions), it will still put the BBC at a relative financial disadvantage in securing access to rights and, more significantly, talent. Potentially, this could damage the quality of the BBC's output and therefore its ability to adequately fulfil its public service objectives. This problem is further compounded by the increasing cost of acquiring rights and securing talent, see Figure 3.2.

In the pre-satellite broadcasting market of several years ago, the scarcity of spectrum gave much of the market power to the few broadcasters that existed. However, as the number of delivery mechanisms for broadcasting increased, so the market power gravitated away from broadcasters and towards key talent who could then increase their prices. This change is clearly illustrated in the case of Premiership football rights. As competition from new broadcasters to secure these rights increased, so their price escalated. Now, instead of the economic rent being captured by

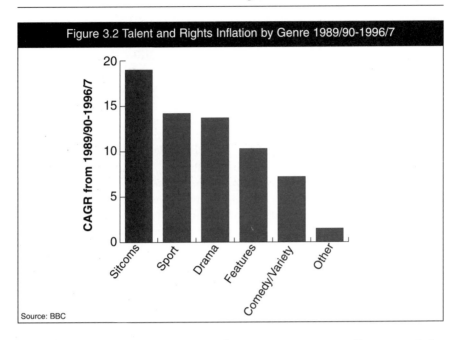

Figure 3.2 Talent and Rights Inflation by Genre 1989/90-1996/7

Source: BBC

broadcasters, as was previously the case, it is primarily secured by footballers whose wages have risen significantly in recent years.[5] In more general terms, the increase in the number of broadcasters has increased the competition for rights and driven up the price of both acquiring those rights and accessing talent. Therefore, the ability of the BBC to earn additional income is important in ensuring that it can continue secure the rights to the best productions and key talent which the viewers and listeners have come to expect.

Securing access to the best available talent for licence fee payers is helped not only by the income that commercial activities generate but also by the exposure that selling programme rights abroad can offer. In other words, both on and off screen talent are more likely to be attracted to programmes that will be broadcast in a number of countries. The BBC have cited Robert Carlyle, the star of *The Full Monty* who worked on the BBC productions *Hamish Macbeth* and *Looking after JoJo*, and Colin Firth, star of *Pride and Prejudice*, as examples of this.

3.2 The criteria for public service broadcasting

The case for the BBC engaging in commercial activities is therefore strong. But where is the boundary between public service and commercial activities to be drawn? What are the criteria for determining whether a BBC product is to be free, paid for from the licence fee income or paid for as a commercial service? This is a difficult area, and one where hard distinctions are difficult to draw, requiring judgement in their application. But three criteria seem critical.

The first is that of the underlying public service mission 'to educate, inform and entertain' in a way that sustains the sense of broader community in British society. This suggests that educational, news and documentary programmes fall clearly within the public service brief. High quality entertainment, that is inclusive and builds the sense of community awareness, is also clearly included.[6] This is clearly subject also to these programmes being generally available, and not simply an elite offering. However, this qualification itself needs qualification: if new technologies are being introduced, it makes sense for them to be adopted for public service offerings even when adoption is limited, because they may well become the future general technology. To stand aside from the internet, for example, because it is only accessed by the few would be rather like the BBC standing aside from television in its early days or from colour television at its inception. Of course, if the internet were not to become widely adopted, then its public service role may need reconsideration, but that will take a decade or so to determine.

Second, there is the need to maintain the integrity of the BBC's role and brand. This has several aspects. Obviously the BBC will not wish to enter commercial areas that are unrelated to its core activities. While its high brand profile might well be useful in, say, selling electricity or cars, the resulting dilution of its brand and the risks of severe damage to its reputation would not justify this. As importantly, the BBC should avoid commercial activities that sully the BBC's brand. This requires the BBC to maintain oversight of its commercial activities to avoid potential damage to its reputation, a point to which we return in section 6. But sustaining the integrity of the BBC's role goes wider than this. It would clearly undermine the BBC's public service role if all, or most, of its major productions were broadcast commercially before being broadcast free-to-air: licence fee payers would rightly question whether the BBC was fulfilling its public service remit.

Third, there is the economic criterion of the cost structure of the service being provided. As discussed above, services with high fixed costs and zero or low marginal cost fit better the public service role, whereas charging for usage is more suited to commercial delivery.

Clearly these criteria need judgement in their application, not least in weighing one criterion against another when they point in different directions.[7] They should be operationalised in the management structure of the BBC, a point to which we return in section 6. They also need to be communicated as a rationale for what the BBC is doing, a point to which we now turn.

3.3 Communicating the rationale

The rationale presented above offers a compelling case from the licence fee payers' perspective for the BBC's commercial activities. However, difficulties are likely to be encountered in convincing all sections of the public that commercial income is a necessary part of supporting public service broadcasting. As the BBC's commercial activities expand and the number of available delivery mechanisms increase, the boundaries between them and core, publicly funded services could become blurred. For example, viewers will find themselves paying to receive broadcasts that are or were broadcast by the BBC. Having already paid for the programme through their licence fee, viewers may question why they should pay for it again. This point was recently illustrated by the case of the TV show *Dad's Army*, repeats of which were being shown both free-to-air on the BBC and through the subscription channel UK Gold. Further questions are likely to arise regarding why particular channels should be commercially funded and others publicly funded. For example, the BBC already operates Internet sites some of which are commercially funded and some of which are publicly funded.

As these types of occurrence become more common licence fee payers may increasingly question both the role of the BBC's commercial activities and, more significantly, the justification for the licence fee. It is vital for the BBC to address these perceptions by communicating the rationale for commercial activities clearly and concisely as an important part of its strategy. However, in addition to this, it will also be able to explain clearly the rationale (discussed above) for determining which services are funded by the licence fee or grant-in-aid and which via commercial income.

The case for commercial activity is a robust one that should stand up well to scrutiny and be persuasive enough to convert the majority of licence fee payers. In particular the trends represented in Figure 3.1 are fundamental. In any other business, a company that projected revenues represented by the lower line, against the background of the rising total revenue line, would most likely become increasingly marginalised. There is no reason to suppose that broadcasting is much different. This key point deserves to be much more widely understood.

Of course, once this case has been clearly recognised, the debate is likely to shift to question how effective the BBC is at maximising the value of its assets in the market. If it is too successful, competitors will seek to use competition law to issue fair trading challenges or to launch a competitive counter-thrust to take some of the value that the BBC has created. If it performs badly, licence payers can justifiably claim that their funds are not being used to their full. We return to the issue of trading performance in section 5.

3.4 Conclusion

The BBC has supported its public service programming with commercial income since the launch of the *Radio Times* in 1923 and the Charter granted to it in 1996 affords greater scope than ever before to develop commercial operations and international broadcasting. Over the next few years, the BBC is faced with a broadly flat income from the licence fee, the increasing cost of

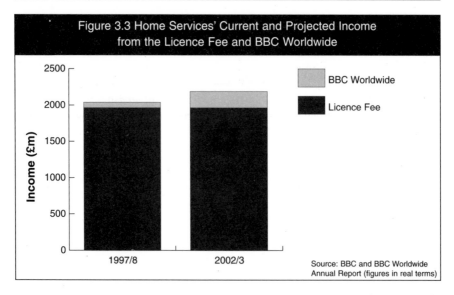

Figure 3.3 Home Services' Current and Projected Income from the Licence Fee and BBC Worldwide

Source: BBC and BBC Worldwide Annual Report (figures in real terms)

acquiring rights and talent, and new challenges presented by digital technologies. Against this background, commercial income will become increasingly important in achieving the standard of programming that viewers and listeners have come to expect of the BBC, as well as in contributing to a flourishing secondary market in the BBC's archive from which it would be wrong for the BBC to remain aloof. It should be seen as a priority and responsibility of the BBC to realise the full potential value of the assets and intellectual properties funded by the licence fee. The increase in opportunity for the BBC to earn commercial income should see more funds being reinvested in free-to-air broadcasts to the benefits of licence fee payers.

4 Constraints on Commercial Activity

As the BBC seeks to maximise the value of the licence fee by exploiting the greater commercial freedom afforded to it, it must do so subject to a set of constraints contained in the Royal Charter and the accompanying Agreement. These constraints are intended to act as a safeguard against the dangers that face the BBC, as a public service broadcaster, in developing its commercial operations. For example, if licence fee money was used to fund a commercial venture, competitors of the BBC could justifiably claim they were facing unfair competition while viewers and listeners could claim that their money was not being used for free-to-air programming as intended. In this section, we examine these constraints and also the procedures for monitoring them.

When considering the constraints that apply to the commercial activities of the BBC, through BBC Worldwide and Resources Ltd, it is important to recognise that they are subject to the same domestic and EU competition laws and regulations as all other UK companies. However, whereas for other companies, these statutes represent the full extent of their constraints, the BBC's commercial operations face further regulation. This additional regulation, imposed by the Charter and Agreement, is in recognition of the unique issues that arise from the nature of the BBC as a licence fee funded, public service broadcaster. For example, there is a possibility of commercial activities being cross-subsidised by licence fee funds or exposing those funds to increased risk. To safeguard against these and other problems, the BBC has to comply with additional regulations, which we now consider.

First, in recognition of the sensitive issues surrounding the commercial activities of the BBC, the Charter gives the Secretary of State the ultimate sanction over them. Although Worldwide has general powers to carry out commercial activities all new commercial services need the Secretary of State's approval. In all instances the BBC is ultimately accountable through the Charter and Agreement for the proper conduct of its commercial activities, with particular regard to the separation of commercial services from licence fee funded activities and for fair trading.

The main requirements imposed on the BBC's commercial activities are published in its document 'Fair Trading Commitments' which also outlines its responsibilities to licence fee payers and competitors. The three main objectives identified in this publication are for clear criteria to be established for all of the BBC's commercial activities, for fair competition in all markets and for no risk to be passed to the licence payer. We consider each of these criteria below.

4.1 Clear criteria for the BBC's commercial activities

The criteria for commercial products and services, outlined in the BBC's *Commercial Policy Guidelines*, require that they:

- plainly arise from, support, enhance or extend BBC programming;
- and add to viewer and listener choice by widening the range and reach of programmes and related products, or programme themes.

The purpose of establishing these criteria is to ensure that the commercial activities reflect the core values of the BBC through their quality, distinctiveness and integrity. The types of products and services deemed suitable are listed as books, videos, audio cassettes and magazines based on programmes or programme themes, merchandise linked to programme titles, themes and characters, the sale of programmes internationally, the operation of international television channels and new interactive multi-media products based on programmes. These are all expected to offer the consumer value for money and to uphold accepted standards of decency.

Whilst these criteria appear exacting it should be noted that they are guidelines published by the BBC themselves and are not clauses of its Charter. The Charter lists a variety of media that can be produced, commissioned or distributed by the BBC provided those activities *'be conducive to any objects of the Corporation'.*[8] Given that clause 3(c) lists commercial services as an objective, this does not impose a strong constraint *per se*. However, although these criteria are self-regulatory guidelines, that is not to say they are ineffective. The principle behind them is that the commercial products and services, which are intended to increase the range and reach of programmes and their related products, should mirror the core values of the BBC. If they deviated from these values it would be to the detriment of the BBC's reputation, brand and ultimately its core public services, particularly in the case of domestic activities.[9] It would only take a few cases of inappropriate products being issued to increase the clamour to remove the licence fee. As the licence fee provides the BBC with its unique position in the UK broadcasting market and currently 97 per cent of the funds spent on its public service programming, its own interests are best served by ensuring that its commercial activities reflect the values of its public service programming. This can be achieved through making the senior management responsible for commercial operations fully aware of the importance of the public service objectives and core values of the BBC.

Although not part of the Charter or Agreement, there is no reason to believe that the self-regulatory criteria established for commercial activities – that they arise from and support public service programming without damaging the core values of the BBC and its brand – would be contravened. It is in the BBC's own best interest as a public service broadcaster to ensure that its core values and objectives remain at the heart of the organisation and that its commercial activities neither damage nor detract from them.

4.2 Fair competition in all markets

In operating both commercial and public service activities, there is the possibility that income from either the licence fee or grant-in-aid could be used to support commercial operations. This could occur through providing investment capital, supporting initial operating losses or commercial services being purchased by the BBC's public service operations at prices above the market rate. However, the BBC's Charter and Agreement prohibit such cross-subsidies. Therefore, in order to ensure the income intended for public services is not used to support commercial activities, the BBC funds, operates and accounts for them separately. The requirement to prevent any cross-subsidy is reflected in the four principles of fair-trading that the BBC has committed itself to and which we discuss below.

- *Arm's length trading relationships* In order to facilitate fair-trading and enable effective monitoring of commercial activities, clear boundaries are drawn between them and the BBC's public service activities. In the case of key commercial activities these boundaries are created through establishing separate subsidiaries, ie BBC Worldwide and Resources

Ltd, whose accounts are independently audited. Other less significant commercial activities are reported in separate trading accounts. Operating at arm's length, in this way, enables costs and revenues to be monitored and appropriately allocated. However, where commercial and public service activities coexist in the same directorate, as in BBC News, it is not easy to allocate costs precisely between the two with complete confidence. Indeed, both accountancy experts and economists would acknowledge that there can be a high degree of arbitrariness in the allocation of costs to products produced jointly.[10] Although it is important to invest time and effort in allocating these costs – to protect against accusations of unfair trading or cross-subsidisation – too much effort can be devoted to this task, ie there will be diminishing returns in the accuracy of cost allocation relative to the cost of the allocation exercise itself. This is not to say that commercial activities within such directorates should not be completely ring-fenced, as significant efficiencies would be lost, or that separate trading accounts should not be compiled but that inefficiencies could arise from this monitoring.

- *Transparent trading and contracts* With boundaries in place between commercial and public service activities, formal contracts and service agreements are used to govern relationships between the two. Making transparent the terms and conditions of trading facilitates the collection of information and the comparison with the terms and conditions that prevail in the external market. The ability to undertake such benchmarking is essential in demonstrating that the BBC is trading fairly – the results of some benchmarking exercises are discussed in section 5.

- *Fair prices* Establishing arm's length relationships and transparent trading conditions are necessary steps in ensuring that the BBC's commercial products and services are sold at a 'fair price'. Obviously, setting a fair price is important for a number of reasons. For instance, if one of the BBC's commercial divisions was selling to the BBC's public service arm at a price significantly above that prevailing in the market it is effectively being cross-subsidised. Further, if the prices charged by the BBC in the open market were below the prevailing level then competitors could use this to argue that it is abusing a dominant position – this is particularly relevant in some of the markets of BBC Resources such as the provision of large studios. The pricing guidelines issued by the BBC require that prices should not be set below marginal cost and that they should make a contribution to overheads.[11] In addition, they should not be significantly out of line with those in the market and prices charged to external customers should be similar to those charged internally. Adherence to these guidelines should guard against any accusations levelled at the BBC that its is abusing a dominant position or cross-subsidising its commercial activities. Naturally, within these pricing guidelines, it is important that commercial activities earn an adequate rate of return within a reasonable time scale. If an adequate return is not earned, then the BBC would once again open itself up to criticism, and probable legal action, on the grounds of unfair trading. This problem has been recognised in the BBC's commercial policy guidelines as financial and operating targets, which are dependent on the nature, risk and investment requirements of the project, are expected to be agreed in advance of new commercial activities being pursued. One of the key factors in setting these targets is the time period over which an adequate return is expected to be earned. In particular, it is important not to have a time horizon that is too short as, although it might be possible to earn an adequate return in the short term, revenue might be maximised by foregoing this in favour of larger returns over a longer time horizon.

- *No unfair cross-promotion* The final key principle adopted by the BBC to ensure fair trading, and reflecting an undertaking given to the Office of Fair Trading, is that there should be no undue promotion of commercial products on core public services. Again, on the grounds that it could offer an unfair advantage through cross-subsidising adverts, promotion of commercial activities on the public service are restricted to short trails at the end of programmes regarding the availability of related products. Commercial products are only mentioned within programmes when it can be justified on editorial grounds.

With adequate monitoring of the adherence to these four key principles, an issue we discuss in section 4.2, the BBC can be confident that it has done as much as is feasible to ensure its commercial activities are trading fairly and are not being cross-subsidised with licence fee funds.

4.3 No risk to the licence payer

The final criterion established in the BBC's Fair Trading Commitments is that its commercial activities should not expose licence fee funds to risk. The main effect of this criterion is that the BBC's commercial subsidiaries cannot secure borrowing against the assets generated from the licence fee and grant-in-aid. The capital they can raise for investment purposes is therefore limited to that which is secured against their assets (but still limited to the £200m external ceiling fixed in the Charter), retained income and, most significantly, that which they can obtain from joint venture partners. Although this criteria might inhibit the ability of the BBC's commercial subsidiaries to maximise the return on licence fee funded assets, it helps ensure, in conjunction with the fair trading provisions, that licence fee funds are only spent on the core public services. The principle of arm's length relationships provides the ability to monitor adherence to this criterion.

4.2 Monitoring procedures

The constraints placed on the BBC's commercial activities, which we have discussed above, are only as effective as the procedures for their monitoring and reporting, and so it is these we now examine.

As part of their regulatory responsibilities outlined in the BBC's Royal Charter and Agreement, the Board of Governors is required to ensure that commercial activities are funded, operated and accounted for separately from public services. This function not only involves the Governors checking that the above guidelines are adhered to but also reviewing the guidelines to ensure they are effective in achieving their objectives. Given the nature of this role, a sub-committee of the main Board of Governors takes responsibility for it - the Fair Trading Audit Committee. The committee meet on a regular basis to ensure fair trading procedures, which the Executive Committee is responsible for implementing, are complied with and management is appropriately addressing fair trading issues.

In fulfilling its regulatory requirements, the Fair Trading Audit Committee receives information from a number of sources. In each directorate and commercial subsidiary a fair-trading representative implements and monitors fair-trading procedures. These representatives report indirectly, through the Chief Adviser, Commercial Policy, who co-ordinates their work, to the Fair Trading Audit Committee on a variety of issues including the results of market testing and benchmarking, on the existence and robustness of contracts and the transparency of accounting between internal and external revenues. This information is augmented by regular reports prepared by the BBC's Head of Internal Audit and by ongoing auditing of compliance by external auditors, KPMG.

On the basis of the information it receives from both internal and external sources, the Fair Trading Audit Committee reports its views on the BBC's compliance with fair trading guidelines in the Annual Report and Accounts. In addition to the opinion of the Governors, external auditors, KPMG, provide an independent view on adherence to the principles that is also published in the Annual Report and Accounts.

5 Activities and Performance of BBC Worldwide and BBC Resources Ltd

In keeping with the principle of arm's length relationships, the BBC has two subsidiaries through which its main commercial activities are managed. These are BBC Worldwide and BBC Resources Ltd. Below, we discuss the activities of these two companies, the income they have generated from external sources and the contribution they are expected to make looking forward.

5.1 BBC Worldwide

Worldwide was established as a subsidiary of the BBC in 1994 to operate the diverse range of commercial media interests that the Corporation had developed. Its main aims are to maximise the value of licence fee funded assets for re-investment in free-to-air programming subject to fair trading conditions and the maintenance of the BBC's core values. Towards this aim, it earned revenue of £409m in the 1997/8 financial year and was able to provide a positive cash flow to the BBC of £75m over the year.

Table 3.2 Breakdown of BBC's Worldwide's Revenue (1996/7)	
By type of business	
UK Books, Videos & Audio	£78m
UK Magazines	£118m
International Programme Sales	£115m
International Publishing	£17m
Channels	£22m
New Media	£4m
By geographical market	
United Kingdom	£214m
Americas	£38m
Rest of World	£102m

As table 3.2 shows, BBC Worldwide operates many types of businesses across the globe. However, its main activities are in UK publishing and international programme sales that together accounted for 88 per cent of its revenue in 1996/7. In both of these businesses, BBC Worldwide performs relatively well. For example in 1996/7, including £27m of co-production funding, BBC Worldwide's revenue from programme sales was £142m. This compares to combined revenue in the same year from the three main distributors of ITV programmes (Brite, CTE and ITEL) of £68m. BBC Worldwide's revenues from programme sales make it the largest exporter of English language programmes outside America - the largest US studios (Time Warner, Disney, Universal and Paramount) had an average revenue in 1996/7 of £1,900m driven principally by the sale of movies to TV broadcasters. In addition, the growth achieved by BBC Worldwide in programme sales in given geographical markets is outstripping the overall rate of growth in those markets. For example, between 1991 and 1996, Worldwide's compound annual growth rate was 9 per cent in America compared to 6 per cent for the US market as a whole. Similarly in Australia, Worldwide's annual growth between 1991 and 1996 was 16 per cent compared to general market growth of 8 per cent. A similar scenario is witnessed in the markets in which BBC Worldwide operates across the globe.

UK publishing, which is Worldwide's other main source of revenue, has also exhibited strong growth. Taking Worldwide's magazine interests, the last 3 financial years have seen sales revenue increase from £105m to £130m, an annual compound growth of over 11 per cent, while the growth in profits and contribution has been even greater. However, revenue growth has lagged behind that of major competitors in this market (Emap and IPC). In the case of consumer publishing, having under performed in 1996/7, 1997/8 witnessed revenue growth of 19 per cent. This growth resulted, in part, from the successful development of cross media brands such as the *Teletubbies* (books, videos, audio, music and merchandising), Michael Palin's *Full Circle* (books, videos and audio) and *Wallace and Gromit* (books, videos and merchandising).

In addition to increasing its revenue, greater reinvestment in public service programming can be delivered through Worldwide finding efficiency improvements. Part of the pressure for achieving these efficiency savings arises through the benchmarking and market testing that is required as part of the BBC's fair trading commitments. The BBC's Rights Agency, which sources and negotiates co-productions deals and licences rights, market tests the investments offered by Worldwide and an independent benchmarking exercise, using data compiled by KPMG, has been developed in recent years. The results of these exercises has been to show that on average Worldwide's investment per hour is broadly in line with that in the rest of the market. Not only does this show that Worldwide is complying with its fair trading requirements, it also suggests that by being able to offer the same investment level as other distributors it is achieving equal success in exploiting the value of the rights. This is achieved in spite of the fact that it is subject to a variety of constraints, in respect of the BBC's public service role and fair trading conditions, which other distributors are not subject to and which, it could be argued, puts it at a comparative disadvantage. Although for some programme genres the investment per hour falls below the rate offered by third parties, this can usually be attributed to programmes having a UK orientation, requiring extensive editing to suit international markets or lacking a demonstrable track record.

Over the five years up to 31st March 1998, Worldwide's revenue has grown at an annual compound rate of over 12 per cent to £409m. This has enabled £75m to be reinvested in the BBC's public service programming - representing a contribution from commercial activities of approximately £3.50 for each £91.50 colour licence fee. The financial targets set for the next five years require revenue to double and the benefit to the BBC of Worldwide's activities to treble. The ambition behind these targets is for Worldwide to become a leading global multi-media organisation and the BBC's strategy for achieving this relies on the following three themes:

- to continue to launch international channels;
- to identify brands that can be developed across media and world markets;
- to continue its performance in core businesses of publishing and to build a position in new media.

This strategy, already being pursued by Worldwide, represents a change from previous practice. In particular, it involves moving away from simply selling programme rights to developing joint venture domestic and international channels. A number of factors influenced this change of direction. The most significant of these is that over the long term, developing channels offers a superior return compared to providing programmes for other broadcasters. Although in the short run a greater return might be earned from simply providing content, as a channel gains audiences so its profits increase. Therefore, over the long term, developing channels is likely to provide greater returns to licence fee funded assets by retaining more of their value within the BBC for the licence fee payer. However, the greater return that channel operation can earn over programme provision comes with greater risk. As the commercial activities of the BBC must not expose licence funds to risk and because of the borrowing constraints that Worldwide faces, finding partners to develop these channels forms an important part of the strategy. Whilst the BBC can provide the partnership with high quality programming and a strong brand, joint-venture partners provide investment funds. This helps the BBC minimise risk from operating channels while still providing it with the associated greater return. A final advantage of developing international channels is that it helps build the strength of the BBC brand in international markets to the benefit of all its other commercial activities. The pursuance of this strategy is demonstrated by the deals agreed with Discovery Communications Inc. and Flextech Plc. and, although the returns will accrue over the longer term, they should go some way in helping Worldwide meet its stretching targets.

The other key aspect of Worldwide's strategy lies in the development of brands across media and geographical markets. This strategy builds on one of the key competitive advantages that Worldwide possesses namely the diversity of its activities. Worldwide operates across some 10 sectors and in 45 countries and, although this could present some management difficulties, it offers a very strong position from which to develop brands. Again, although in its early stages, this strategy is already being pursued as witnessed by the success of the *Teletubbies* and Michael Palin's *Full Circle* brands across a number of media. Going forward, the newly established Global Brand Development division will seek to increase the amount of revenue and profit earned from abroad by such cross media brands. The ability to develop a portfolio of world-wide brands across different media is a potentially huge source of commercial revenue that could be used to support public-service programming.

5.2 BBC Resources Ltd

As part of the Producer Choice reforms in 1993, which introduced an internal market into the BBC for the provision of resources and services to programme makers, BBC Resources was established as the owner and manager of all technical, craft and support services in the BBC. Even though over capacity had been reduced and working practices improved before its creation, BBC Resources had clear incentives to further eliminate over capacity and operate as effectively as possible as its income was now earned on a commercial basis rather than from the centre. By 1996/7 annual savings in BBC Resources were estimated to be running at £120m per annum. However, despite becoming more competitive, its share of the internal market has continued to decline to its current 1997/8 level of 68 per cent. Over the next 5 years internal demand is forecast to decline between 4 per cent and 6 per cent per annum, largely as a result of advances in technology such as lightweight digital cameras and non-linear editing. This erosion in the internal of level demand would represent a significant cash drain for the BBC if allowed to continue.

To address this situation, in February 1998 the Board of Governors approved a proposal to allow BBC Resources to expand its external trading. In keeping with fair trading commitments, this involved the incorporation of two thirds of BBC Resources assets into a wholly owned commercial subsidiary while the remaining assets, which have little or no potential to be traded externally, would be placed in a new directorate, Production Services.

Looking forward, over the five years to 2002/3, revenue from external trading has been forecast to increase from £32m to £97m, an annual compound growth rate of 21 per cent. In addition, cost savings of 22.5 per cent have been factored in over the period. If these targets are achieved then BBC Resources Ltd will move from being a cash drain to generating cash and pre-tax profits ready to be reinvested in public service programming. Whilst these targets appear ambitious, in 1997/8 income from external trading increased by 31 per cent over the previous year to £34m. The potential revenue to be earned from external trading, particularly in the corporate and on-line/multimedia markets, make these targets realistic.

6 Organisational Issues

The analysis of the previous sections has put the case for the BBC developing its commercial activities alongside its key role in public service broadcasting. This raises some important organisational and management issues. Should the commercial activities be managed alongside the public service activities, or should there be organisational and managerial separation?

There is a strong case for separation of the commercial parts of the BBC, as has been done with the incorporation of BBC Worldwide and BBC Resources as distinct corporate entities but wholly owned by the BBC. There are several reasons for this. In terms of fair trading conditions, it will be easier for a separate corporate entity, with its own accounts, to furnish persuasive evidence that it enjoys no cross-subsidy from the public purse. Because of this, it will be able to pursue commercial objectives more aggressively without fear of falling foul of competition law. It is therefore more likely to enjoy commercial success, to the benefit of the licence fee payer. This point is reinforced by the fact that the management style and organisational culture required for successful commercial ventures are likely to differ markedly from those needed for pre-eminence in public service broadcasting. This points to the need for separation, both organisationally and managerially, of the two activities.

However, there are also good reasons for not allowing a complete separation as would occur with the sale of the BBC's commercial activities. The synergies between the commercial and public service activities are appreciable in a number of areas, and complete separation would deny the opportunity to derive the benefit of these synergies. Complete separation could put at risk the valuable BBC brand. Moreover there is an important commonality of strategic purpose between the commercial and public service activities. Thus the commercial part has a strong interest in innovative and successful BBC productions that can be spun out into the commercial marketplace; while the rest of the BBC has a strong interest in a flourishing commercial arm that can leverage productions commercially, with earnings flowing back to enhance the BBC's public service role.

What is the best way to balance these two sets of considerations? Several elements are required.

First, what is needed is the formal separation of the commercial activities through the creation of wholly owned but separate corporations. This allows the appropriate distinctive managerial styles and organisational cultures to develop in the public service and commercial parts of the BBC, free of the need to compromise the two parts.

Second, there needs to be effective oversight of the commercial activities by the senior BBC management and the Governors, to ensure that the commercial activities do not compromise the BBC brand and are synergistic with the overall objectives of the BBC. To be effective, this oversight needs to be light-handed and operated within clearly defined principles. What needs to be avoided is micro-management of the commercial activities, since this will undermine their capacity to operate in the fleet-footed and flexible way essential to commercial success. Devising arrangements that gives this is not straightforward, and there may be adjustments to be made to current arrangements to enhance the BBC's governance of its commercial activities.

Finally, there needs to be a recognition in both the commercial and public service parts of the BBC that, though their objectives differ, they also overlap. Thus the commercial and public service parts share important strategic objectives, and their trading relationship should reflect this.[12] Thus relationships will not simply be confined to haggling over the price of the service to be delivered (which is essentially a zero sum game between the two parts of the BBC, in which one side benefits only at the expense of the other), but will extend to discussions of how the relationship can develop the capacity of both sides to meet their distinct, but overlapping, strategic aims (which represents a positive sum game in which both sides can benefit). This may best be accomplished through a strategic partnership that identifies common strategic interests, acknowledges divergencies of interest, and formulates a medium strategy for working together in those areas where collaboration gives benefit.

Such a strategic partnership does not undermine the drive for efficiency provided by the discipline of the internal or external market. Many commercial companies find it advantageous to form strategic partnerships with other companies to pursue joint interests, but do so with a strict eye on the bottom line.[13] If such arrangements are advantageous in pursuit of profit, they can also be advantageous in pursuit of the BBC's public service mission.

7 Conclusions

The BBC's role as a public sector broadcaster has continued, indeed enhanced, relevance in the new digital age. With its positive mission to 'inform, educate and entertain', it acts as a centre of quality that helps sustain the quality of commercial broadcasting, and averts the real risk of a rush to the bottom that may well happen in a purely commercial broadcasting market. The quality of British television and radio attests to this.

The BBC has engaged in secondary commercial activities from its beginning, and these activities are set to expand. These activities represent a key support to this public broadcast role. These commercial activities ensure that licence fee payers get the full value for money by deriving a secondary commercial stream of income from the secondary exploitation of BBC productions. Not to exploit these commercial activities would be a scandalous act of negligence on the part of the BBC, not acting in the best interests of licence fee payers. Given political resistance to raising the licence fee much ahead of inflation, the additional commercial income provides for the BBC an important source of growth of real income. With total spending in the industry set to rise sharply with the launch of multiple digital channels, this income growth is key to the BBC's ability to maintain its pre-eminent position in the industry.

The general case for the BBC's commercial activities is therefore unassailable. However, the combination of public sector and commercial activities within the BBC does raise more detailed issues that have to be addressed.

First, with this combination, the BBC finds itself uniquely constrained: on the one hand, to account for the proper use of public sector funding (both licence fee for domestic broadcasting and grant in aid for the World Service); and on the other to ensure that it complies with general competition law, and is not cross-subsidising commercial activities from the licence fee. These constraints, and the resulting need to be seen to be whiter than white, impose on the BBC the need for complicated accounting separation procedures that certainly reduce the scope for efficiencies in the organisation as a whole. It seems to us that the rules on public sector funding could be interpreted more liberally without putting at risk the licence fee payers' interests. But that is a matter for Government, not the BBC.

Second, there is the question of the criteria on which different activities are categorised as public service broadcasting to be met from the licence fee and as commercial. Two main criteria seem relevant. First there is the economic question of whether the service entails high marginal costs of delivery, in which case a commercial charge and commercial delivery seems more appropriate; or high fixed costs and zero or low marginal cost, more appropriate to public service delivery. Then there is the question of whether the service meets the public service criteria, and in particular the needs to educate and inform and to help shape and sustain the sense of wider community. It is not easy to interpret these criteria in a hard and fast way, partly because the nature of community is likely to evolve as is the adoption and impact of new technologies. But this does not take away from their importance and the role of public service broadcasting in preventing a lowering of standards.

Third, there are the organisational and management issues associated with the combination of both public service and commercial activities in the same organisation. Success in the commercial sphere may well require quite different skills from success in the public service sphere. For that reason, it is important that the two sets of activities are separated structurally within the BBC. This has been achieved through the internal market and the incorporation as wholly owned subsidiaries of BBC Resources and BBC Worldwide. It is also important that management of the two parts is separated, so that the different management styles and cultures required for success in the two spheres can be developed. On the other hand, it is important that the two sets of activities do not grow too far apart, with separation and sale of the commercial activities as the logical end result. Since the aim of the commercial activities is to leverage the public service role, this would be an unsatisfactory outcome, and moreover one that might risk the BBC's valuable brand. What is required is the recognition, through a strategic partnership between the public service and commercial arms of the BBC, of the interdependence and the appreciable alignment of interests and strategic objectives between the two. Such partnerships are common in the commercial world, and are often key to corporate success.

Managing these issues is not straightforward, but nor is setting the right strategic direction in the new digital world. The BBC is right to pursue its commercial activities alongside its public service role. These activities provide a key element to ensuring that the unique pre-eminence of the BBC, both in the UK and overseas, and its association with quality and objective reporting is sustained.

Notes

1   BBC's Annual Reports and Accounts 1997/98, Chairman's Introduction.

2   For a full discussion of these issues, see chapter 1 by Andrew Graham.

3   See Graham. This argument is not that market and commercial forces necessarily neglect quality: such a proposition is clearly false, as can be seen in other consumer markets where an emphasis on quality and service delivery is usually the key to commercial success. Rather the proposition is that the particular features of the broadcasting market, both on the supply and demand side, mean that market forces left to themselves without a corrective are unlikely to work well.

4   However, this is set to fall over the next five years as revenues from commercial activities contributes increasingly to the growth of budget of the Home Services; see Figure 3.3.

5   For further details see Cowie, C. and Williams, M. (1997) 'The Economics of Sports Right', *Telecommunications Policy*, 21(7), August, pp. 619-34.

6   It is important to appreciate that the sense and definition of community may well evolve, so that what falls within this category will change over time.

7   The first two would seem more fundamental than the third.

8   BBC Charter, clause 3(l).

9   This is less of an issue for Resources Ltd, who arguably derive less benefit from the BBC brand, than for the publishing and broadcasting activities of BBC Worldwide.

10 Consider the allocation of costs between licence fee and grant-in-aid for BBC World Service. Take, for example, the production of a news item for BBC World Service. Suppose that there are resources in BBC News (funded from the licence fee) that are currently available to be deployed to enhance the quality of the BBC World Service item, with no detriment to BBC News activities. With costs allocated on a conventional, average cost basis, this may not be possible because this would imply a cross subsidy from licence fee to grant-in-aid activities. But economic analysis would suggest that resources that are currently available have zero or low marginal cost. Valued accordingly, their use would imply no cross-subsidy. Similar issues arise in the allocation of resources between licence fee funded activities and commercial activities. A great deal also depends on how marginal cost is computed.

11 As we have already noted, much depends on how marginal cost is calculated.

12 This point and the following ones apply equally to trading within the BBC internal market between the different BBC divisions within the BBC (eg Production and Broadcast), as BBC policy and practice has increasingly recognised.

13 See Doz, Y. and Hamel, G. *Alliance Advantage* (Harvard Business School Press, 1998) for a recent discussion of strategic alliances and what is needed to make them work well.

Chapter 4

Competition and Public Purpose: a European Approach

Graham Mather

What is society looking for in public service broadcasting? In Britain we have tended to arrive at an answer by a process akin to osmosis. Beneath and beyond the vigorous discussions enjoyed by broadcasters are some implicit assumptions which from time to time are crystallised by political pronouncement or codified in regulatory decisions.

The implicit terms for a ten-year renewal of the BBC's Charter in 1996 were that it would provide a wide range of services at the higher end of the quality scale in its various markets, at a level of productivity which kept the licence fee within reasonable bounds and that it would be sufficiently commercial to achieve these results without engaging in anti-competitive practices which seriously disconcerted its commercial rivals.

These objectives – imprecise and requiring careful balancing judgements – seem nonetheless to reflect a broad national consensus, both popular and political. The BBC has an ethos, a scale and a track record which defines for itself a model of public service broadcasting which continues to satisfy national taste and temperament.

It is clearly these factors which led the government to confirm that there will be no full scale review of the BBC's purpose and governance until 2003-4, and that the licence fee review to be conducted in 1999 will start from the position that the licence fee model itself is sustainable until the renewal of the Charter.

I believe that this approach broadly reflects public opinion at the end of 1998. Yet five years is a very long time for which to lock in a particular structure, especially if it is one arising out of a national tradition which relies on shared assumptions rather than clear institutional structures. Across Europe legal and regulatory initiatives may, at least, require codification of the British assumptions and test whether they resolve the potential conflicts between audiovisual, public service, state aids and general competition policy which this paper will attempt to unravel.

Before doing so, however, it would be wise to examine to what extent the assumptions which underlie British public service broadcasting will be challenged by commercial rivalry, technological change and the new economy of converged information industries.

1 Commercial Rivalry

Scarcely had the Secretary of State finished delivering his keynote speech setting out the broad lines of Britain's broadcasting future[1] than the BBC was outbid for test match cricket transmissions by Britain's other broadcaster with a complementary public service remit, Channel 4. The decision not to outbid Channel 4 was defensible as a commercially-informed decision based on prudent stewardship of licence-payer resources. Yet it generated a rather adverse media and public response. It put in a stark light the Culture Secretary's suggestion that 'What [the BBC] needs most to retain public confidence is to continue to be true to its distinctive public service ethos and programming range. That way, it will continue near universal reach and its near universal public respect'.[2]

Put another way, near universal reach and hence respect may depend on a deeper purse: or at least access to other sources of finance which so far have not been available to the BBC. The universalist assumption in the mind of many British policymakers is that a basic entitlement for citizens is 'a variety of quality programmes which speak to their day to day concerns, which keep them informed and entertained, which offer everything from the undemanding sheer entertainment of popular soaps and game shows to challenging, innovative drama and documentary'.[2]

The requirement that the BBC continue to 'provide something for everybody, making the good popular and the popular good' is demanding in terms of quality. It is still more demanding in financial power if it transpires that access to the largest-audience football, boxing and cricket events must be provided on free to air channels and that access to these must be bought in the open market against competitors offering focussed pay TV channels.

Sport has been the most dramatic example of the broader issue and these challenges make it urgent to find a durable means of defining the public service remit, as well as to identify acceptable ways to supplement the licence fee.

2 Technological Change

The arrival of digital television imposes a further requirement for rapid policy development. The prevailing assumption is that of the Culture Secretary, that 'I continue to believe that the large majority will continue to rely for some time to come on more or less traditional, one to many, scheduled broadcasting services for most of their entertainment and information needs'.

If this language means that there will be no dramatic adjustment to financing or regulatory systems until around the time of the BBC's Charter review in 2003-4 this may be about right. Yet the margins will be tight. The signs are that new technology will catch fire quickly and widely once technologically advanced, accessible and well-priced new platforms become available.

In particular digitalisation of telephone systems is in my view likely to lead to a significant growth in web television. As a result the delivery over the Internet of broadcast-quality sound and moving pictures, currently in its early stages, could well increase exponentially. As an OECD study in 1997 noted, 'close and informed observers of the Internet in both the research and corporate communities estimate that full real-time voice and video capabilities on the Internet will probably be available within three years.'[3] European Commission experts also expect a rapid transformation, envisaging within five years 'an Internet with 100 times current performance/cost levels in throughput and speed to the final user. Telephone would become a by-product with a few cents per minute only even for trans-Atlantic traffic. Nearly unlimited distribution capability for television or other video products from distributed video servers via the Internet may become available.'[4]

The BBC's website, BBC Online, is the most-used content site in Europe and has reached 30 million hits per month with a growth rate of 30 per cent per month. Sir John Birt has said that it may become a highly significant medium for the delivery of the BBC's public service proposition.[5]

3 Content Changes

Digital technology and the spread of the Internet has two far-reaching consequences highly relevant for Europe's public service broadcasters.

The first is that it will make it possible for quite small producers to deliver content to broad audiences via the Internet as easily as large traditional broadcasters, without the dedicated infrastructure of large studios, transmitters, terrestrial or satellite delivery technology.

The second is that it will lead to a globalization of delivery and an evaporation of traditional regulation. If it is impossible to regulate the Internet other than through a new pattern of self-regulatory communities, parent choice and technological facilities it will no longer be viable to attempt to run a parallel system of content regulation for traditional broadcasting. A critical question for regulators and the BBC alike is whether this development will have occurred in five years or fifteen years time.

Content is what matters. As Ted Turner has put it, 'There are lots of conduits but there's only one *Gone with the Wind*, one *Casablanca*'.[6] The strength of the BBC is its programmes. As digitisation of content production and delivery develop this distinction and a consequent focus on quality of programming will come into sharper relief. It will create new requirements for regulatory systems which can cope with contestability from more providers and a multiplicity of channels and platforms.

4 EU Tension

It is at the level of the European Union that the tensions between broadcasting and competition policy are becoming acute and need to be resolved.

In a last minute addition to the Amsterdam Treaty, now being ratified, member states agreed some 'interpretative provisions' designed to prevent Community law from inadvertently damaging the ability to shape public service broadcasting arrangements at national level.

Alas, however, these interpretative provisions are themselves open to different interpretations.

The Protocol[7] says that Treaty provision are without prejudice:

> ...to the competence of Member States to provide for the funding of public service broadcasting in so far as such funding is granted to broadcasting organisations for the fulfilment of the public service remit as conferred, defined and organized by each Member State, and that such funding does not affect trading conditions and competition in the Community to an extent which would be contrary to the common interest, while the realization of the remit of that public service shall be taken into account.

This splendid piece of Europeanese manages to beg the key question: is it a particular type of public service broadcasting or trading conditions and competition which is most in the common interest of the EU? If the answer is that the two must be balanced, against which criteria and in what forum will the balancing adjustment take place?

4.1 Court of Justice

As long ago as 1991 this debate on state aid entered the legal arena of the European Community when the Spanish television company Telecinco lodged a complaint against regional broadcasters and the public service broadcaster RTVE.

Four other cases are currently pending, in Italy, France Germany and in the UK from BSkyB. The cases all revolve around allegations that public service broadcasters have a protected position and are able to compete unfairly against private sector competitors.[8] Frequently the problems arise from the fact that public service broadcasters are allowed to take advertising income: Figure 4.1 shows the wide variety of sources of funding for European public service broadcasters.

In September 1998 the Court of Justice censured the Commission for failing to take a decision on the Telecinco case. As a result the Commission came

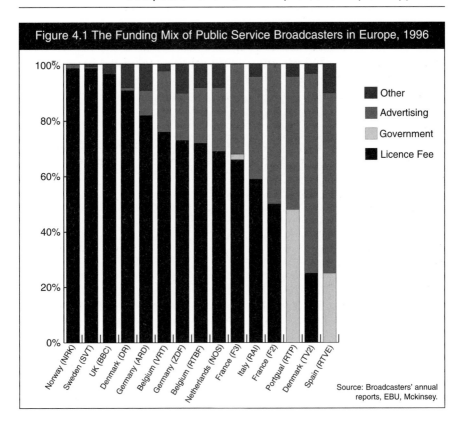

Figure 4.1 The Funding Mix of Public Service Broadcasters in Europe, 1996

Source: Broadcasters' annual reports, EBU, Mckinsey.

under pressure to take more speedy and decisive action in relation to complaints, forcing a more speedy and comprehensive debate about the relationship between support for public service broadcasters and general competition policy, as well as between the powers and responsibilities of member states and the European institutions.

4.2 Two key principles

These cases require balanced solutions which pay respect to two principles. The first is that public television plays a vital role in most Member States of the Community, a fact which has recently been acknowledged in the Amsterdam protocol. The second is that European economic integration is rooted in competition and the free market. The future of Europe's distinctive 'dual' public/private broadcasting system depends on these two apparently incompatible principles being reconciled as far as possible.[9]

In calling for 'certain basic principles and funding criteria' to be drawn up, the expert group set up by Commissioner Oreja set out some basic tests:

The funding of public service broadcasting must:

- Be in proportion to, and not more than, what is required to discharge the public service remit (the criteria of proportionality).

- Be granted on open terms such that compliance with this principle can be checked on at any time (the criteria of openness).

- A public service broadcasting remit may be entrusted to public or private sector operators, as each Member State chooses.

- When there are public and private sector operators on the market, there must be safeguards to ensure fair competition.

- Each Member State must therefore define clearly, in its national legal system, the scope of the public service requirement and the specific obligations in terms of programming and other requirements associated with it.

- To ensure compliance with the criteria of proportionality and openness, public sector funding must be provided exclusively for broadcasters with a public service remit as defined by each Member State.

- For this purpose, financial openness should be applied, in particular where a public service operator receives funding from sources other than public sources in the realisation of its public service remit. Furthermore, when that operator engages in purely commercial activities (ie that go beyond those activities defined as being part of its public service remit) separate accounting should apply. This is necessary to avoid public sector funds being diverted to commercial activities.

- Taking account of the specific situation in each Member State, the funding of public service activities should come mainly from public funds; recourse to the advertising market should remain secondary.

These recommendations provide a balanced approach which many in both public and private sectors will find acceptable in principle. It is in the detail that the challenges of definition will apply.

5 A New European Framework

And as the debate moves to the details, it is possible to agree straightaway with two propositions emerging in the EU approach.

The first is that most European citizens want the best of both worlds in their broadcasting: the best traditions of public service broadcast and the availability of strong private sector offerings. Both may achieve high market shares and have powerful market presence. To some extent technology will determine the pace of change to a massively multiplied choice for consumers, at which point the durability of financing and regulatory models will be tested. But for now, as a recent European Commission study noted:

> Given the current level of concentration in the sector, the level of fixed costs (eg for the acquisition of rights, etc) and the dimensions of the major private players in the market, such pluralism and neutrality of information can, nowadays, be ensured only by the presence of efficient and technologically advanced public broadcasters.[10]

It is an acceptance of the approach which has informed the BBC's development of its 'implicit contract' with the public and the rapid expansion of its worldwide web, news and information offerings.

The second point of agreement is on the need for public sector broadcasters to behave commercially. Shielding public service broadcasters from the incentive to innovate, adapt leading edge technologies, and pioneer at the sharp end will in the long run damage themselves, their public service role, lead to ever increasing requirements for state support and unsustainable licence fee demands whilst lack of the latest content and technology would lead to a reduction in market share greater than the secular trend.

5.1 The tension between national preferences and European state aid policies

The potential tension between the wish to allow public service broadcasting to fulfil its full potential in member states, capturing the history, culture, preferences and ethos of a society and acting as a reference source and a pointer to the future, and the general rules of European competition and state aids policy is profound.

If general rules on state aids were followed in the broadcasting sector, for example, public service broadcasting would not exist, and if competition rules alone were pursued many public service broadcasters would fall foul of abuse of dominant position rules, for example in respect of lack of access for competitors. There would be difficult discussions about frequency allocation and the extent to which it might favour incumbent or public broadcasters.

The concept of public service broadcasting and the elimination of state aids and promotion of competition come from different traditions. As a recent European Commission study noted, 'Competition law is not the right vehicle for achieving cultural or regulatory aims.'[11] There is a further deep set of distinctions between the preferences which inform public service broadcasting in different member states. This may make it of little utility simply to collect the definitions of public service broadcasting favoured at member state level.

Such definitions are likely to be advanced at a high level of generality, to be vague, to allow maximum discretion for the member state in using state funds to support its broadcasting, and to be too imprecise to check and measure against competition law.

The requirement to achieve a resolution of the dialectical contradictions between national public service remits and competition law cannot be long delayed because of the range of complaints which have been made by private broadcasters. Against what tests should the European Commission and the European Court of Justice seek to resolve these issues?

6 Which Approaches Will Work?

Three main conceptual approaches could achieve at European level the balancing which this chapter has explored.

6.1 Tenders

The most frequently proposed 'free market' solution is the public tender approach. States would define a public service remit and invite organisations to bid for its supply. The best package is chosen, the member state reimburses the extra costs of providing the defined service, and subject to satisfactory clarification of the financial relationships between public service and other broadcasts in terms of advertising, sponsorship and the avoidance of cross-subsidy Community competition and public procurement rules are complied with.

It is an approach already used elsewhere in Community law. Yet the tender approach, whilst possessing many merits, may be inadequate. Its appeal is that it may toughen up charter or licence renewal procedures which assume the continuation of an existing incumbent supplier. It could establish benchmarks in a competitive environment and put a premium on fresh thinking. The alignment with the takeover threat, common to large private sector companies, is a powerful and constructive discipline.

The tender system would also fit with other aspects of new social governance. Public procurement rules across the European Union enforce this contestability already. Next Step Agencies, which cover the overwhelming part of the operational functions of British government, are also subject to quinquennial review at which an examination is made as to whether the agency should be privatised, placed on a trading fund basis, otherwise restructured or left in place.

A tender system need not be 'all or nothing'. Provided that financial separation and transparency is in place, particular aspects of the public service remit could be bid for by new potential suppliers in much the same way that the internal market already operates within the core BBC.[12]

But for all these apparent advantages the tender system might in practice prove too rigid to capture the fluid and difficult-to-define boundary of the public service remit, which is something of a discovery process. There is a national interest in maintaining a critical mass of production excellence which could be lost in a tender system. Some of the pressures which a tender system would bring to bear already exist: the 25 per cent quota required to be provided by independent producers is a clear example.

There would be problems of definition of boundaries. A tender system might, to take another example, lock BBC Online into the public service function when on reflection it turned out to be a powerful new platform in which BBC products could, because of the nature of the Internet, be supported by advertising without detriment to the public service remit.

There would be a rigidity which could limit the ability to use a public service or commercial arm as was most appropriate.

A tender system would put great significance on the specification of the public service remit itself: something which, as argued above, may be difficult to achieve with precision. National policymakers would be reluctant to lose flexibility in defining the core public service role, whilst the pace of technological change and content innovation could make a standard tender period of say five years seem lengthy.

Clearly a tender system which transferred to civil servants the task of defining the remit and choosing the content would be fraught with potential difficulties. A system which intruded deeply into programme making would be unlikely to be acceptable.

6.2 A dual system

More complicated than a tender system, but perhaps more intuitive and familiar, is the dual system which prevails in many member states in Europe, and which has led to the complaints from private broadcasters of an unfair competitive regime.

Under this system public service broadcasters are able to obtain sponsorship and advertising and also receive a licence fee or other state support for the public service parts of their service.

The question which must now be addressed is whether this model, reformed to seek to make explicit and transparent the relations between public service and commercial activities, is capable of providing a robust and durable way of ending the tensions which are leading to current difficulties across Europe. It is immediately obvious that such a system would pose enormous practical, legal and regulatory complications.

A dual system would need to reflect and accommodate different concepts of what public service broadcasting amounts to – a matter which the Amsterdam Protocol highlights is dependent on national, regional and cultural traditions and preferences. Yet to ensure fairness to broadcasters across Europe this decision must comply with the pan-European model which regulates monopoly public services across the utilities: the concept of general economic interest, which became a significant legal concept in the Treaty of Amsterdam. It is an imperfectly formed concept, vigorously promoted by French nationalised public utilities, which allows competition rules to be bypassed when operators meet some rather ill-defined standards of universal service. The principle is broadly that the public policy case for the service is so essential that its very existence should not be called into question by competition policy.

It is unsurprising, therefore, that as well as cutting across national preferences the general economic interest model runs up against other Treaty provisions promoting competition and contestability in public service. This would make it difficult to define public service broadcasting widely, would run up against European Court of Justice jurisprudence in competition policy and state aids.

Even if these obstacles can be overcome the dual system involves ferocious practical difficulties in measuring and allocating costs and allowable reimbursements. These would mean that the European Commission would achieve enormous power over the structure of financing and programming.

The dual system would mean, for example, that in order to make sure that covert subsidies were not passing to broadcasters who had inflated the cost of providing public service programmes the Commission, in the absence of competition, would invoke a system of 'proportionality', scaling back 'non-proportional' State funding in excess of what it deemed to be necessary.

It would also mean that the Commission could have to act as policeman of the boundaries of the legitimate remit of public service broadcasting. Once again, its decisions would be likely to fly in the face of national preferences. Sport provides a good example. The Commission could seriously restrict any attempt to treat sport as a 'licence fee' area, and could impose rigid and somewhat arbitrary tests around precisely which fiction, serials and films could be considered of a public service character. The attempts to make these distinctions and separate out the related costs in every member state in the European Union would be both intrusive and unworkable.

The effective removal of many sporting broadcasts from the BBC would run directly counter to the advice of the Select Committee on Culture, Media and Sport, which in its recent report directed some sharp criticism at the BBC's loss of rights to broadcast some major sporing events.[13] It was less clear, however, whether the Committee attributed this to shortcomings of negotiation or lack of resources and if the latter from where they were to be provided. The Committee's suggestion that 'the forthcoming review of the BBC's funding should examine the scope for commercial partnerships as a means of supporting BBC acquisition and retention of sports rights in future' begs the question of fair competition. It could lead straight into the circular argument that existing resources need to be expanded, licence fees alone cannot take the strain, commercial money is needed but this combined 'state funds plus' approach should not be used to compete unfairly with market providers.

6.3 Split financing

The solution to these problems is in the third possible model of public service broadcast finance, one in which revenues are split – advertising revenues to commercial operators and licence fee or other State revenues exclusively to public service broadcasters.

Under this option Britain could choose to retain a licence fee to support core BBC public service channels and services, whilst allowing and encouraging the BBC to compete vigorously with private operators in the marketplace.

The BBC itself has begun to go down this road. It has separated some commercial activities into BBC Worldwide Ltd, a wholly-owned subsidiary which is operated at arms length from its parent with important safeguards. BBC Worldwide pays the BBC for commercial rights to programmes at market rates which are benchmarked and does not borrow more money from the BBC than its own net assets. It is also subject to the BBC's Fair Trading Commitment, which requires transparent contracts and fair prices for BBC services and programmes.

Are these arrangements sufficiently firm, well-established and independently policed to form the basis of a new structure in which the BBC became both a state-supported and a commercial broadcaster, with the government able from time to time to adjust the boundary between market and state-supported elements?

They broadly meet the letter and spirit of the European Commission's draft guidelines, which favours the split approach because it means that state-funded broadcasters would not be allowed to compete directly with market operators on the advertising market, thus limiting possible distortions in trade, although the state support would help secure audience in a manner potentially detrimental to the non-supported operators. At the same time the split system would connect public broadcasters to the incentives and innovations of the market but with proper safeguards for competition: 'Public broadcasters may, of course, compete on the market, but only through dedicated channels or subsidiaries, which would not receive direct (eg funds not at market conditions) or indirect (eg programmes not at market conditions) from the public service entity.'[14]

6.4 Designing the ideal model

The split financing system has all the benefits of clarity and transparency. Across Europe it provides much the most straightforward way to separate the commercial and public service elements of state-supported broadcasters without creating arbitrary definitions in advance. It gives the state the flexibility to define the services which it wishes to support, whilst separating these from activities which are competing directly in the open market.

The split system would go with the grain in Britain, as it builds upon the way in which the BBC has attempted to separate its commercial functions from the core public funded areas.

To work, however, the new system will have to be built upon some robust transparent and justifiable rules, first in the drawing up of the dividing line between public service and commercial functions, and secondly in the establishment and policing of contractual and pricing relations between the BBC and its commercial arm.

Drawing the dividing line is made easier because the split financing system does not limit the public service remit to services not provided by private operators. Instead it allows governments or regulators to continue to support the distinctive approach to broadcasting which is the public service role whilst not competing unfairly with the commercial market. As public funds are finite, there is a built-in incentive to shift relevant services to the commercial arm, and expose them to competition in so doing.

In both cases the establishment and policing of competitive behaviour can be done along lines similar to those which would be followed by regulators of privatised public utilities. Broadcasting will become less of a one-off, immune from the usual rules and procedures of regulated markets. As it converges with other forms of communication its institutional structure can be brought into line with other services providing universal services to the public, the services known in the EU as services of general economic interest.

7 Summary of Conclusions

Europe's systems of support for public service broadcasting are running counter to European competition law because they fail to distinguish sharply enough between state-supported public service remits and the commercial activities and in most cases advertising income of state broadcasters.

Competition law cannot be applied across the board to broadcasting issues because of different national and regional cultural preferences.

Complaints which have been hanging fire since 1991, a delay condemned by the European Court of Justice, make it essential for the European Commission to provide a methodology to allow these problems of state aid and distortion of competition to be resolved.

Three potential solutions are examined in this paper:

- The first, a tender system for public broadcasting would be clear but inflexible and at odds with the dynamics of the development of modern innovative public service broadcasting.

- The second, a dual model in which state broadcasters could run public service and commercial roles within the same structure, would create impossible boundary problems and could also lead to bureaucrats making programme decisions.

- A solution is available in the third model, a split financing system in which state support can only go to public service broadcasters whilst advertising sponsorship or commercial income can go only to a commercial operator (which may be a commercial subsidiary of a public service broadcaster with adequate regulatory checks) would solve these problems, maximise transparency, and increase competition whilst giving governments an incentive to curb the licence fee.

In the UK the BBC has already moved in this direction with its commercial subsidiary BBC Worldwide and the more robust regulatory system to police the boundary of public service and commercial broadcasting is heralded in the Competition Act 1998.

Notes

1   14 October 1998, Royal Television Society Autumn Symposium.
2   Rt Hon Chris Smith MP, *supra*.
3   'Content as a new growth industry', *OECD Working Paper* 46, 1998.
4   Speech by Herman Ungerer, European Commission DG IV, Paris, 14 May 1998.
5   Select Committee on Culture, Media and Sport, Eigth Report, *The Report and Accounts of the BBC for 1997-98*, 5 November 1998.
6   *The Times*, 6 November 1998.
7   'Protocol on the System of Public Broadcasting in the Member States', *EC Official Journal* C340/109.
8   Mediaset v RAI (Italy) TF1 v France 2 and France 3 (France) VPRT v Kindercanal and Phoenix (Germany) SIC v RTP. Further complaints have been submitted to the Commission recently.
9   Report from the High Level Group on Audiovisual Policy, EU DG-X, 27 October 1998.
10   'Application of Articles 90(2), 92 and 93 of the EC Treaty in the broadcasting sector', DG-IV Discussion Paper, October 1998.
11   Wachtmeister, A-M , *Broadcasting of Sports Events and Competition Law*, DGIV Competition Policy Newsletter June 1998.
12   1997/8 was the first full year in which broadcast and production were separated, with BBC Production being obliged to compete with other providers.
13   Select Committee on Culture, Media and Sport, Eighth Report, *The Report and Accounts of the BBC for 1997-98*, 5 November 1998.
14   DGIV Discussion Paper, *supra*.

Chapter 5

Broadcasting and Public Purposes in the New Millennium

Julian Le Grand and Bill New

1 Introduction

The BBC's Royal Charter specifies that its task is 'to provide, as public services, sound and television broadcasting services.... and to provide sound and television programmes of information, education and entertainment for general reception in our United Kingdom of Great Britain and Northern Ireland'. Since this document – along with the accompanying Agreement between the Secretary of State and the BBC – is subject to regular parliamentary scrutiny, especially when the licence fee is up for renewal, they can be taken as representing a kind of implicit contract between the BBC and its audience, the licence fee payers. Not surprisingly, the nature of this contract is not always as clear as it might be. But it is apparent, both from these documents and from the way in which the BBC has evolved over the years, that the prime purpose of the BBC is to respond to the needs and wants of its funders, the licence fee payers. Moreover, it is also clear that the BBC is not supposed to be an arm of the state, a mouthpiece of government or even a crude instrument of social engineering, moulding society according to an agenda solely dictated by government.

However, the use of terms such as 'public service' or 'audience need' suggests that there is a sense of social purpose that underlies its activities, as does its role in providing information and education. The BBC is a major institution of British society and therefore has to respond to social needs as well as individual wants. But what form should this sense of social purpose take? There is no one objective definition of social purpose or indeed of 'need' or of 'public service'. Rather the interpretation of terms such as these will vary, as society's wider concerns vary. Hence the BBC has to devise appropriate responses to those changes in social concerns so that it can better reflect the society of which it is such an important part.

Just such a change in social concern is under way at the moment. The 1960s and 1970s were a period of what might be termed old–style social democracy: a time when the dominant philosophy was egalitarian, economically interventionist and socially liberal. The 1980s and early 1990s were the heyday of economic liberalism: state intervention in the economy was reined back, individuals' economic rights were emphasised, although – somewhat paradoxically – social liberalism was increasingly deplored. The election of the Labour Government in May 1997 reflected in part a further shift in the value base of society; one towards what one of the authors (Le Grand 1998) has termed CORA: Community, Opportunity, Responsibility and Accountability. It is with the implications of such shifts for the BBC that this paper is concerned.

The paper begins with a discussion of the four principles of community, opportunity, responsibility and accountability, and how broadcasting as a technology – however financed – contributes to CORA objectives. Then we analyse why a purely private market might fail to achieve these objectives, before turning briefly to the question of whether these objectives could be satisfactorily achieved through regulation rather than subsidy. The following section looks at the stated aims of the BBC – both in published documents and as expressed by senior personnel[1] – and how well these match up to CORA principles. Finally we turn to a discussion of some of the issues raised in earlier sections, including the difficulties involved in broadcasters pursuing social objectives, some issues of BBC accountability, and the challenge of the multichannel era. There is a short concluding section.

2 The CORA Principles and the Potential Contribution of Broadcasting

In this section we introduce the four principles in general terms and then examine how broadcasting as a technology can contribute to their realisation. We should make it clear, however, that we are not personally endorsing these principles. Rather, they represent, as it appears to us, the current realignment of political values in late twentieth century Britain.

2.1 Community

If the 1980s was the era of rampant individualism, the 1990s may go into history as the decade when the importance of communities and of communitarian sentiments was re-discovered. Now support for the ideal of community, and to the associated ideas of co-operation, consultation and partnership, can be derived in part from a belief in these ideas as *means* rather than *ends*. The view is that in certain areas of society, especially those traditionally associated with the public sector such as health, education and local services, employing communitarian methods of doing things is simply a better way of achieving broader social goals, such as greater social justice and economic efficiency, than individualistic competition.

Competition is seen as fragmenting services, as setting public sector professionals and managers against one another, as impeding sensible planning, and as fermenting inequalities. Further, many of the social problems with which governments deal are viewed as multi-dimensional and as requiring a co-ordinated, communitarian approach to resolve them. The emphasis on local communities, in particular, also reflects in part a concern with means or process; local communities are viewed as being better placed to resolve local issues than the national government.

However, community is seen as not only a means to an end, but also as a valuable end in itself. Societies where individualistic competition is king are peopled by aggressive, adversarial individuals; people who are unpleasant to meet socially, to have more intimate relationships with and indeed even to work with. Further, as the communitarian philosopher Amitai Etzioni has argued (1993), individualistic societies are also likely to be places where people insist on their 'rights', often at the expense of others, and, more generally, at the expense of the common good. Moreover, they will see these rights, not as privileges accompanied by responsibilities, but as unconditional; rights-driven individuals are often reluctant to accept that the realisation of their rights is only possible if everyone behaves responsibly. Thus a universal 'right to a public education' or to 'quality health care' can only be fulfilled for everyone if people are responsible about paying the taxes that finance that education and health care.

In contrast, communitarian societies are much more agreeable places in which to live. The formation of community ties between people makes them happier and more fulfilled. Interpersonal relations, of whatever kind, are more enjoyable if the individuals concerned are not always trying to compete with one another, or perpetually asserting their 'rights'. Further, a society where people willingly meet their responsibilities has a higher quality of life than one where people continuously try to evade them. A functioning community also provides its members with reassurance; others will be there to help if they hit hard times.

A broadcaster can act as an instrument for promoting community as a social end – a sense of community in the wider society – in a number of ways. First, it can allow a large number of people to share in consumption of a single product at the same time. There are relatively few goods or services outside broadcasting where it is possible to jointly consume in this way – a large rock concert or football match involve many thousands of people in the audience, but do not match the millions who regularly tune into soap operas and share the developing storylines on a daily basis. This, so the argument goes, provides a means of promoting a more integrated national community. A large number of people sharing in the same activity gives a sense of social purpose and cohesion (Kumar, 1986). This phenomenon goes beyond those programmes where millions of people simply watch at the same time, to include 'landmark' broadcasting which binds the national community, such as the England football team's matches in the World Cup, and the reaction to the death of Diana, Princess of Wales.

A second way in which broadcasting can promote community is through education. If society is indeed fragmenting, with polarised ethnic and religious groups for example, then there needs to be some means of preventing this diversity turning into conflict. Divergent values must be able to co-exist in a society if it is to function well. Both political parties have in recent times articulated such a desire: John Major's society 'at ease with itself' and Tony Blair's 'inclusive' society. Broadcasting can illustrate how a successful society depends on mutual respect and tolerance. It can also show what happens when communities lose respect, or fail to understand, one another – as, for example, with the graphic broadcast images of the inner city riots in the early 1980s which provoked a reassessment of race relations and policing in the UK.[2]

Finally, broadcasting can provide a foothold in society for the marginalised. An increasingly important core value for society is that no member of society should feel 'excluded', whether they are unemployed, single parents, lonely pensioners, even abused children. This does not necessarily imply higher material standards of living for these groups. But it does require that they should all feel they have some stake, that they are important and have a legitimate point of view. No-one should be left behind by virtue of their circumstance, lifestyles or the unfortunate choices they might have made in the past. Broadcasting is perhaps uniquely placed to respond to those who might otherwise be marginalised, by acting as a forum for their concerns and desires, and by helping them to feel part of society – partly by being able to share in 'landmark' events and even soap operas. It may also allow them to develop pride and self-respect, and strengthen their own community ties. This may suggest local broadcasting if the community is focused in a particular geographical area, or national if the excluded community has a 'interest' unrelated to a particular area.

2.2 Opportunity

Opportunity is an important ingredient of current values in two respects. First, maximising opportunity per se is thought to be desirable. The good life should not be prescribed; people should not have the decisions that affect their quality and enjoyment of life made for them, but should have the opportunity to make those decisions for themselves. Everyone should have the opportunity to maximise their own potential.

Second, opportunity is the conceptual method by which egalitarian considerations are respected. Many theorists now endorse equality of opportunity as the relevant egalitarian aim, often explicitly rejecting the apparent alternative of equality of outcome as a desirable goal in and of itself (although they may accept greater equality of outcome as instrumental – see below). The aim is not to equalise individual outcomes, but to give everyone the same opportunity to maximise their potential.

Everyone should be given a chance to acquire income, wealth or other elements of the good life, but should not necessarily be provided with those elements directly – and certainly not equally.

Opportunities do not, of course, depend only on skills. They also depend on availability of options, knowledge concerning that availability and, to some extent, on preferences. So, for instance, you cannot take up an opportunity to go to college if there are no places available, or if, because of discrimination of one kind or another, you are prevented from taking up such places as are available; if there are places available but you do not know of them; or if the only known places available are in courses very low on your list of preferences. The last point is perhaps the most contentious, because it implies that people do not always know what is in their best interests – young people should be rather more enthusiastic to go to college than they in fact are. However, it seems at least plausible that we do not always fully understand the long term benefits which education might provide, or indeed how much we will actually enjoy college life once we begin.

It should be clear from the above that promoting equality of opportunity or maximising opportunity is not simply about outlawing unfair discrimination or the provision of facilities for the disabled, but also about education in its widest sense: education that provides skills, education that imparts knowledge, and education that creates 'educated' tastes. In all of these areas broadcasting can play a role.

First, in a straightforward sense broadcasting can provide the means for facilitating the acquisition of skills. Numeracy and literacy, as well as more advanced skills, can be made accessible to wide range of people – the Open University, for example, was designed specifically to make use of broadcast media. But educational objectives can also benefit from technology. Graphics, in particular, can be brought to life using audio-visual techniques. Where very specialised equipment is required, such as scientific machinery for the Royal Institute lectures, broadcasting can make it available to a wide audience. Broadcasting here promotes opportunity by encouraging the acquisition of skills in order to make the most of innate abilities.

Second, broadcasting can widen those opportunities that depend on knowledge. This differs from conventional education in that there is no particular 'skill' being taught. Instead, knowledge and information may be an important element of programming where the primary purpose is not educational. Put simply, broadcasting offers a window on the world and reveals what is possible. It is difficult to make a decision about a holiday, leisure activity or career – about what interests or skills one *might* have – without first being presented with the practical possibilities. In this sense, broadcasting again occupies a unique position; for no other means exists of bringing such a wide range of experience into people's homes, with such immediacy and vibrancy. Simply switching on the television or radio transports us across the world, or into a classic drama, or just into an interesting conversation about a subject we had never previously considered. Broadcasting is particularly well suited to this because it is so accessible – we can genuinely fall into new knowledge by accident. 'Channel surfing' may have acquired a bad reputation – the dwindling attention span of modern men and women – but it is also a means of revealing the enormous variety of life's possibilities.

Third, broadcasting can educate our tastes, thus broadening our opportunities by opening up new avenues of enjoyment and fulfilment previously judged to be 'not for us'. This happens in two ways. 'Classic' works of art or entertainment which were previously the province of an elite, or of previous generations, can be presented to new audiences – classic literary texts or old black and white films, for example. Or it can present innovative, daring and risky formats and talent, thus challenging us to develop 'preferences' we did not know we had. Neither of these possibilities is unique to broadcasting. But because of its accessibility it can present previously elitist material in a new light. Similarly, the new and risky have a greater chance of success because a wide spectrum of viewers and listeners are more likely to 'stumble' across something they did not believe they liked on television and radio, than they are to leave the comfort of the living room in order to discover it for themselves.

2.3 Responsibility

The notion of opportunity is closely linked to that of responsibility. If two individuals are faced with the same opportunities to make money (in the broadest sense: that is, they have the same skills, knowledge etc, as well as not being discriminated against), then each is responsible for their own outcome. If one chooses to avail themselves of those opportunities while the other does not, then the resultant inequality of income is of little concern. Indeed, this is the reason why equality of outcome is rejected as an aim: for it denies the concept of personal responsibility.

But responsibility does not derive only from equality of opportunity. For the implication is not just that people facing equal opportunities are responsible for any differences that may ensue between them; it is that even when opportunities are unequal, those faced with the smaller opportunity set cannot use that as an excuse for passivity. The fact that a school is in a poor area does not justify poor examination results; for some schools in poor areas get very good examination results. Everyone is responsible for such exploiting such opportunities as they have open to them.

The role of broadcasting in promoting responsibility is rather more limited than that for the other CORA objectives. This is because, at best, the degree to which people act in a responsible manner is only indirectly affected by what they watch on television or listen to on the radio. After all, unlike community and opportunity, responsibility is not something that people generally desire for its own sake. It may be indirectly attractive to people because they realise it reflects a position of power or importance, or because they enjoy acting 'morally'. But, in general, it restricts our freedom to act as we wish, and is thus not directly in our self-interest.

But it would also be easy to underestimate the role of broadcasting. The Right has always argued that the BBC partly encouraged the permissive revolution in attitudes to sex, drugs and parenting that developed during the 'irresponsible' sixties. Others have taken a similar line: Mary Whitehouse, when a leading figure in the National Viewers and Listeners Association, blamed broadcasters for many of the perceived ills of modern society, including the exposure of children to sex, and the affect of dramatised violence on levels of crime. The link between screen and real-life violence has in particular spawned a small industry in claim and counter-claim. And the comments of pop stars with regard to drug taking – Noel Gallagher's recent comments in a Radio 1 interview being simply the latest in a long line which started with Mick Jagger – continue to provoke claims that the young will inevitably copy their heroes and engage in dangerous or immoral activities. In any event, the impact of broadcasting on responsibility, or irresponsibility, cannot be ignored.

If so, could broadcasters have a role in a more 'positive' version of responsibility? There are already examples of how such a role might manifest itself. *CrimeWatch* encourages viewers to report criminal suspects to the police – not to 'turn a blind eye'; drug awareness campaigns have been run on Radio 1; and safe sex/HIV storylines have been prominent on soap operas. So in principle broadcasters could encourage nineties–style responsibility, although this might be construed as rather too close to assisting party political objectives, a point we return to below.

2.4 Accountability

Accountability is not so much a final objective, but one derivative from the fact that the government (or society in general) has more fundamental aims to pursue. Instead it is an essential part of any democracy: the set of mechanisms that ensure that a government or its agents achieve whatever ends the democratic process has decided should be achieved. In particular, the agents of the state (professionals, public sector managers, bureaucrats) must demonstrate that what they do is in line with the goals that have been set for them.

Now a vigorous, independent press has long been considered a precondition of a healthy democracy. The investigative journalist uncovering corrupt goings on in public officialdom, or the 'thundering' leader denouncing some aspect of public policy – these are essential elements of a political system which wishes to prevent those in power from abusing their authority. Better government will result from persistent, unfettered criticism.

Broadcast journalism and current affairs programming can enrich this well-established role in a number of ways. To a greater degree than is possible in the print media, broadcasters can seek a 'live' response to a question of public concern, thus allowing the viewer or listener to judge for themselves how the interviewee performs. It is difficult for the guilty to hide; if they do, it is clear for all to see. Thus, the interrogation of government ministers on the Today programme provides an *immediate* form of accountability impossible in print journalism. Public humility is often the result – witness the repeated questioning of Michael Howard by Jeremy Paxman over his part in the resignation of the head of the prison service, or Bill Clinton's travails over what he did or did not do with Monica Lewinsky. These acts of public scrutiny act as a deterrent for others, as well as a means of discovering the truth.

Neither is it just politicians who are subject to investigation: professionals who have stepped out of line, public sector managers suspected of lining their own pockets – even the heads of private corporations giving themselves fat pay rises. None easily escapes the glare of broadcast accountability.

But it goes deeper than simply holding individuals to account. Democracy requires that impartial information is widely and equally available to all, so that the people can make up their own minds about political issues of the day. And it also requires some degree of access so that members of the public can actually take part in the debate, rather than simply acting as passive observers. In both these regards, broadcast media are ideally placed to improve the democratic health of the nation.

Finally, broadcasters need to demonstrate accountability and probity themselves, not just as a public service broadcaster disposing of public money, but more generally as a model of good practice. Institutions which claim to promote accountability, if they are to succeed, must be trusted and respected, not least by those who might be subject to its investigations. Otherwise broadcasters leave themselves open to the charge of hypocrisy. Thus broadcasters must be a model of accountability *themselves* if they are to successfully achieve their wider aims.

3 Why is the BBC Necessary to Achieve CORA?

So far in our analysis we have examined how broadcasting as a technology could potentially promote the ends of CORA. We have done so uncritically: clearly there will be elements of broadcasting which may not be unequivocally beneficial to these ends or indeed other ends of society, and we will refer to some of these below. For now we simply acknowledge its potential for beneficial outcomes. But first we need to establish why the BBC, with its particular system of financing, might be necessary to their full realisation. In other words, why cannot the market, based on advertising or subscription, support CORA on its own?

To some extent, the commercial sector *does* achieve CORA ends. The community objective of mass viewing is at times well served on ITV where the wish to maximise advertising revenues provides the perfect incentive for maximising audiences – *Coronation Street* has regularly achieved the highest ratings in any given week. Furthermore, *The South Bank Show* has been acclaimed for its treatment of the arts – and thus for potentially expanding opportunity. News and current affairs has successfully been provided by ITN and other ITV companies – which would appear to serve accountability.

It is true that commercial services in the UK are regulated for public service ends – for example, the ITC demand quality thresholds for ITV which include requirements for news, current affairs, regional programming and diversity in the service. Nevertheless, the least regulated services – on cable and satellite – provide a 24-hour news channel and educational programming (such as those on the *History* or *Discovery* channels), even though they are under no legal requirement to do so. Furthermore, in other markets consumers wish to be surprised with something unfamiliar every now and then – people don't always choose the same dishes on restaurant menus. And we all 'demand' that our political masters are kept under close scrutiny in the political marketplace. So why is the product of private demands such as these insufficient to maximise the benefit broadcasting can provide?

In fact, in each of the CORA categories there are reasons for believing that the private market will not lead to an optimum outcome. Community may be neglected to the extent that we all benefit over and above the individual value we place on a particular programme. Thus, for events of great importance, the benefit we derive from *national* bonding is in addition to that derived from watching the programme reflecting the event. So, during a General Election for example, a broadcaster should devote sufficiently in-depth coverage properly to reflect these deeper needs of bonding and community. However, for the commercial sector, it is simply the 'watching' benefit which is taken into account and thus it may not supply sufficiently 'intense' programming. In other words, the commercial sector may fail to provide a the right quality for certain types of collective need.

More straightforwardly, commercial broadcasting may on occasion reflect the base instincts of communities, whether they are focused on the cohesiveness of society of not – witness the popularity of 'hate jocks' on American radio. A large proportion of the community – those who are anti-gay, for example – may be strengthened at the expense of a minority. Of course, the acceptability of homosexuality is a political and moral judgement, and broadcasters such as the BBC may feel reticent about taking an overt position on such matters. Nevertheless, simply following the market imperative could damage community relations.

A final element of community which is likely to be less well served by commercial broadcasters is the provision of services for the wide range of interests within it. This is particularly true for low income groups – single parents or the unemployed, for example. Not only are these groups unlikely to offer substantial audiences for programmes which serve their interests, but commercial broadcasters would not be able to command a high price from advertisers because of the disadvantaged groups' low spending power. The BBC can afford to ignore such financial imperatives, and to serve groups such as these.

Opportunity may also be poorly served by purely private exchange. As long as viewers' demands are precisely in line with their actual preferences or needs, then educational and informational programming will be supplied by the market. But there are a number of reasons why this equivalence will be absent. The market will only try to provide the information – the range of opportunities – we, as viewers, think we want. But it is in the nature of opportunities that people need to be presented with them; we do not know what they consist of in advance. Furthermore, we may act with 'myopia' by demanding what will satisfy us here and now, rather than considering how certain types of information may benefit us in the future. In broadcasting, therefore, we will principally demand – through our viewing habits – the set of opportunities reflected in what we *already* know will satisfy our immediate desires. Commercial broadcasters will thus tend to be conservative.

Commercial broadcasting will also act conservatively in providing opportunities for people to develop their tastes. If we, the viewers, know we like a particular range of programmes – chat shows, game shows, films and sport – this is the type of programming which will be supplied. We may not believe we like costume drama or a documentary on political history. This applies to both the range of programming and their formats – changes to a tried and trusted formula will be resisted. We are in general, 'satisficers' not 'maximisers' – we are concerned with simply getting enough, not getting the best. Commercial broadcasters will respond in kind – why should they risk changes that might not work? The BBC can 'afford' to take such risks. Thus, commercial broadcasters may fail to maximise even our short term opportunities.

Responsibility is the third CORA objective that may be poorly served by commercial broadcasters. Again, the market will not take into account the effect of its programmes beyond the individual viewer. So, if violent programmes are extremely popular, but also increase the general levels of violence in society, the commercial broadcaster may only take into account the numbers watching, not the additional cost elsewhere. This is not to suggest that commercial broadcasters are deliberately irresponsible or believe themselves subject to such considerations – and they would rightly point to the inconclusive nature of any evidence proposing a link between screen and other violence. But the point is that the balance of incentives runs counter to restraint. The BBC, on the other hand, does not have the same incentives, and it could take the view that until the argument was resolved one way or the other, it will err on the side of caution.

Finally, accountability may also be underserved. Although we all want our political masters and heads of industry to be held to account, we may not pay for it if we think others are doing so. Everyone gains from successful accountability mechanisms, regardless of whether particular individuals supported them directly. So, if a *Today* programme interviewer interrogates a minister about her poor progress in implementing an election pledge, and if the interviewer succeeds in uncovering poor performance and deters other ministers from doing the same, it is not just the people who listened to the programme who gain. We all do – even those of us who never listen to the *Today* programme. However, a commercial broadcaster must primarily take into account the number who actually watch or listen when deciding the resources to devote to this kind of programming. They may not supply enough to satisfy the accountability which we are in fact willing to pay for, if we could only be prevented from free riding on that minority who actually watch (and thus attract the advertisers).

There is also potential for a conflict of interests in a commercial market. It is less likely that an advertising-financed channel would risk upsetting its paymasters by investigating claims of wrongdoing by a major company which uses its air-time to advertise its product. Thus, whereas the BBC can run a programme such as *Watchdog* which investigates the conduct of major retail chains, a commercial broadcaster would be less likely to risk the potential loss of revenues which might result.

4 Regulation versus Public Service

There is another variant on the issue of the appropriate response to the potential failings of the commercial market. Instead of a publicly owned BBC, why is it not possible instead to regulate the commercial broadcasters to act in the public interest? Compulsory payment of a licence fee would thus be avoided, and public purposes achieved without the political discomfort of justifying a flat rate 'tax'. In fact, ITV is already heavily regulated to achieve many CORA-type aims, and Channel 4's whole licence is determined by precisely the sort of objectives which CORA might imply.

However, there are two significant difficulties with regulation or 'rules-based intervention'.[3] The first is that, given the essentially qualitative nature of public purposes, they are difficult to set out precisely. They require additional judgement about how to achieve them. It will be down to the regulators to exercise that judgement on behalf of commercially funded broadcasters, and to monitor their activities to ensure their compliance – something which will require a significant degree of effort. This is not least because these broadcasters will have an incentive to dilute their public purpose, and concentrate more on programming which will boost their income. It may therefore be more efficient to set up a public body whose whole ethos is geared toward these public objectives, than to police a complex and imprecise set of regulations devised to coerce a recalcitrant private operator.

The second difficulty with rules-based intervention is that regulation typically works well when it is preventing things from happening – such as the broadcasting of explicit sex or excessive violence – but less effective at obliging actions or goal-seeking. This requires *positive* pressure on the licensee to act in certain ways at all times, something which a regulator will find difficult given its arms-length relationship with the broadcaster.

There is, however, an empirical difficulty with these theoretical positions. Channel 4 has, by and large, lived up to if not exceeded its public service expectations. It has been widely seen as innovative and committed to minority interests. And yet it is funded by advertising and run under a set of rules – positively requiring certain types of programme – which were established by an Act of Parliament and policed by the ITC. Does not this 'success story' provide evidence to contradict the theorists?

It is true that the experience of Channel 4 indicates that regulation can achieve more than was once supposed. But Channel 4 is in many ways a special case. It is not privately owned, and thus the imperative to boost revenue is not over-riding. In addition, in its early years, its revenue was guaranteed by the regulator, leaving it further protected from the imperatives of market forces. Latterly, since it has sought to demonstrate it can survive under its own advertising revenue stream, and thus decouple itself from subsidy altogether, the suspicion has grown that its radical edge is blunted. The regulator has even issued warnings that its schedules contained a worrying quantity of American imports. Thus even a non-profit organisation which operates from commercial revenues may be tempted to divert from its public purposes.

Further, it may be that Channel 4 is successful in achieving public service ends, precisely because of the existence of the BBC. Both Channel 4 and the BBC, and indeed the ITV companies and Channel 5, all compete with each other not just on numbers watching, but on the basis of the very public purposes outlined in this paper. This suggests that regulation should complement, not replace, the BBC. In such a system, excessive public ownership is avoided, and the BBC can remain a gold standard by which other broadcasters are constantly judged in delivery of *their* public service obligations.

5 The BBC's Stated Aims

So far we have examined how CORA might be achieved by broadcasting as a technology, and why the BBC might be better placed to achieve those ends than a commercial broadcaster, including those subject to regulation. Now we turn to the question of how well placed the BBC is to achieve those ends. The first requirement is that the stated goals of the BBC are commensurate with CORA, both in terms of written documentation and as a result of interviews with key personnel (see acknowledgements).

First, the Royal Charter and Agreement, which together constitute the principal legal codification of what the BBC should be trying to achieve. The Royal Charter says little of relevance beyond the quote at the beginning of this paper, the key element of which is that the BBC's services should consist of information, entertainment and education, and that they should not be charged for in the UK. Clearly this provides substantial leeway. However, rather more specific obligations are outlined in the Agreement, which outlines the services and standards expected from the BBC by the Secretary if State. This gets closer to public purpose – it requires that the Home Services:

(a)   are provided as a public services for disseminating information, education and entertainment;

(b)   stimulate, support and reflect, in drama, comedy, music and the visual and performing arts, the diversity of cultural activity in the UK;

(c)   contain comprehensive, authoritative and impartial coverage of news and current affairs in the UK and throughout the world to support fair and informed debate at local, regional and national level;

(d)   provide wide-ranging coverage of sporting and other leisure interests;

(e)   contain programmes of an educational nature (including specialist factual, religious and social issues programmes as well as formal education and formal vocational training programmes);

(f)   include a high standard of original programmes for children and young people;

(g)   contain programmes which reflect the lives and concerns of both local and national audiences;

(h)   contain a reasonable proportion and range of programmes for national audiences made in Northern Ireland, Scotland, Wales, and in the English regions outside London and the South East.

3.3   The Corporation shall transmit an impartial account day by day prepared by professional reporters of the proceedings in both Houses of Parliament.

This goes some way to specifying the public purposes of the BBC, and, to a significant degree, it echoes CORA objectives: (b), (d), (f), (g) and (h) relate to community, (c) to accountability, and (e) and (f) to opportunity. Internal BBC papers flesh out this document; *The BBC Beyond 2000* interprets its public purpose thus (comments in parentheses are the present authors' interpretation):

●   to create services of real cultural value (ie to innovate, take risks etc);

●   to offer the UK's most comprehensive source of local, national and international news and information; to be the world's first choice for accurate, authoritative news;

- to provide something of particular value to all the UK licence payers (ie to support diversity and minority communities);
- to support learning (ie educational opportunity);
- to guarantee universal access to services of distinction and quality (ie free at the point of use to all, thus creating as common point of reference, supporting national community);
- to pioneer new technology and to be a trusted guide in a world of abundance;
- to bring benefit to Britain around the world.

Many of these objectives were also reflected in the opinions expressed by senior BBC personnel in interviews with the authors on the nature of the Corporation's public purposes. In particular, there was a strong sense that, because every household pays the licence fee, every household should receive something of value from the BBC. Much effort has gone into understanding the needs, interests and passions of the BBC's audience, to the extent that it has undertaken a highly sophisticated demographic analysis of all the communities of interest which make up its audience. The result is 'The 100 faces of Britain' which, as its name suggests, breaks down the UK population into 100 sub-groups defined by 'lifestage' or categories reflecting lifestyle. The analysis is used better to understand where the BBC is succeeding, or failing, to provide what is wanted by all the various communities it believes it should serve. The value to these 'tribes' offered by the BBC will not derive solely from the main television and radio channels, but will in the future include new digital services, Online Internet access and the use of new technology to offer inter-activity and even to provide information through personal pagers.

BBC personnel also emphasised innovation, taking risks, education and information (a new 'learning' channel is planned for digital transmission), and the central importance of impartial and authoritative news and current affairs, as key elements in the BBC's public purpose. This will now be familiar ground to readers of the earlier sections of this paper. Indeed, these explicit objectives – whether written or spoken – are *prima facie* consistent with CORA principles, and from that perspective at least there is little case for any wholesale change in the direction of BBC policy.

However, the status of CORA as a set of beliefs, the ambiguous nature of the principles themselves and the dawning of the new multichannel era pose significant challenges for the BBC. There are also some areas where we suggest that the principles discussed in this paper have implications for programming policy which are not always reflected in official documentation. These issues are discussed in the final section.

6 Public Purposes, Accountability and the Multichannel Future

It may not be always clear to its viewers that the BBC has a social purpose. To them it is a provider of television and radio programmes to which they watch or listen in large numbers. In fact, in total, people spend more time listening to or watching the BBC than to the output of any other single broadcasting organisation. Leaving aside why, we can at least be sure that the audience enjoys what it sees and hears sufficiently to continue to switch on. Even before the BBC had competition, high ratings would have been enough to persuade many that it was doing something right (people turned to broadcasting rather than other leisure activities). Moreover, in an era of significant choice – much of it freely available to all – the fact that people still predominantly turn to the BBC indicates that it is providing a service of value.

But when 12 million people tune into *Pride and Prejudice* there is, as indicated above, reason to believe that such a success is possible because the BBC is *not* financed on the basis of the numbers of who choose to watch or listen. The market shies away from the production of 'risky' programming – where there is no prior evidence that large audiences wish to watch – which turn out to be highly popular. Filmed classic literary texts is one such genre. As long as the overall benefit from such risky programmes outweighs their cost in the aggregate (including those risks which 'fail'), we all gain. But the key point is that responding to 'needs' rather than expressed wants, is a social judgement – made not on the basis of individual's decisions about their own interest, but as a collective judgement about how markets can fail. The BBC is not simply 'out–competing' its market competitors, but is acting as a public institution with public purposes.

Of course, in other ways the BBC's public purpose is rather clearer, such as its emphasis on educational programming. In this case, the BBC may achieve only small audiences; after all, most people do not need to learn literacy skills. But this will not be considered problematic if the social objective – expanding educational opportunities for those who missed out in the past – does not rely on large-scale consumption. But where significant audiences *are* achieved it may be easy to forget that very often this will be the result of a social purpose to correct a failure in commercial broadcasting, and not simply the BBC out-competing the opposition.

It may be important for the long term sustainability of the licence fee that this point is continually pointed out to the licence fee payer, as a means of retaining political support. The modern citizen is no longer the passive, and grateful, recipient of public services. He or she wants to know why public finance is necessary and what he or she is getting for it. Otherwise, viewers will rightly ask why such highly popular programmes cannot be financed with advertising or subscription.

6.1 Issues surrounding public purposes

The trouble with public purposes is that they are typically less well defined than individual demands. They are not a simple aggregate of the expressed wishes of individuals but a collective judgement on behalf all members of society, in this case the licence fee payers. They are thus often expressed in summary or indicative terms but without the explicit detail which might frighten off those with the least to gain. They are also contestable – that is, they are not politically neutral, or reducible to empirical verification. Thus they change over time according to the moral and political tenor of the time. It is with these types of social objective that the BBC constantly grapples, and to which CORA principles relate. This is as it should be. Nevertheless, there remain a number of issues surrounding the pursuit of principled social objectives by public institutions, some particularly acute for a broadcaster such as the BBC.

First, there is always the possibility that other sets of principles become 'politically' relevant, but which also lend themselves to the public service broadcaster. Thus, a more libertarian government may espouse anti-communitarian principles – that we should each look after our own interests, and the state should avoid any social policy directed at so nebulous a concept as 'community'. Or a neo-conservative government might emphasise national culture and British traditions above all else – thus making an emphasis on the new, innovative and culturally diverse similarly out of touch. This is not to suggest that the pursuit of CORA should be abandoned, merely to indicate that the BBC cannot choose its interpretation of public purpose in relation to one set of political values without acknowledging that these might change and yet stay within the compass of a public service broadcaster.

A second set of issues concern the overall desirability or otherwise of CORA. The very fact that no government document has explicitly endorsed or specified CORA makes them principles which the BBC can safely identify with – there is little chance of the accusation of political bias. But unfortunately this vagueness leaves the precise nature of the objectives open to dispute. Part of the function of this paper is precisely to unravel some of these uncertainties, and it does seem to us that some interpretations of these objectives could have a malign influence on society.

Take community, some of the problems with which were outlined earlier. A more united national community could be encouraged by making programmes which poke fun at foreigners – such as those which ridicule the antics of people in other countries as revealed in their own television programmes. Thus national cohesion is bought at the expense of international antagonism which damages the world community. However, the BBC should take care to avoid such an approach, which can be all too easy to slip into. This may simply be a matter of presentation: a international football match involving home teams could be presented in an unjingoistic manner, thus enhancing the national community without damaging the international one.

However, this relates to a more general problem: how is the proper balance to be maintained between larger and smaller communities, for example between Scottish and British identities? The best way of supporting one community's cohesion might be to encourage it to stand in opposition to another. If this is inappropriate – as we suggest it is – then any form of 'local' broadcasting needs to be alive to the possibility of offending the sensibilities of wider society, and thereby damaging relations more generally.

Community ends can also be obtained by suppressing the rights of individuals. Documentaries on the danger to local communities posed by paedophiles could help bind the majority of that community in opposition to a single individual – who is effectively hounded out and left with no community of their own. In fact, the whole notion of community does not leave much room for the individual who does not fit in, or perhaps holds views reviled by the majority.

These dangers reflect the ambiguity and contested nature of the word 'community'. Similar problems exist with 'responsibility'. A view of the responsible citizen as a gainfully employed, god-fearing heterosexual, could easily be reinforced by stereotypical programming. Although 'opportunity' and 'accountability' appear less controversial at first sight, there can be occasions when the former is aggressively paternalistic and the latter intrusive. For example, educational programmes about good parenting or the 'correct' amount to drink smack of the nanny state; aggressive questions about the private lives of individuals in the public eye take accountability too far.

CORA are thus principles which need interpretation. Some interpretations we believe would be malign; other commentators would not necessarily agree. Nevertheless, adopting CORA as a benchmark for BBC policy requires more than just signing up to the headline principles. In particular, the BBC requires appropriate accountability arrangements to ensure that the chosen interpretation accords with society's prevailing values.

6.2 The accountability arrangements

We have seen how the BBC can act as an instrument of accountability, but it should also be a model of accountability, setting a good example to the rest of society. Accountability in this context is essentially an issue of answering for how public money is spent: how are public purposes decided and how are those tasked with meeting these obligations, held to them? The present government has not established what it believes the BBC's priorities should be – nor would it get very far if it tried. In health or education, on the other hand, the elected representatives are ultimately responsible for what policies are pursued. In health, the Secretary of State can, without invoking new legislation, establish the priorities of the service by means of executive letter or statutory instrument, or by hiring and firing senior managers. In education, especially since the 1988 Education Act, the Secretary of State has powers to amend the national syllabus, as well as sending in hit squads to take over 'failing' schools. Ultimately, in both sectors, if the operation of the public service is not considered to be fulfilling its proper purpose new legislation can be brought in to oblige a shift in policy or behaviour of those working within it. All this unashamedly derives from the authority of a political party in government, using as its legitimacy the result of the previous general election.

The BBC is in a more complex position. Although it is ultimately a creation of the state, it cannot be allowed to become an instrument of a particular political regime in the same way as other public services. Broadcasting as a technology was first recognised as a powerful tool of political propaganda by the Nazis in thirties Germany. One hardly needs to add why such a relationship with the state needs to be resisted in the future. There may be disagreement about precisely how and to what extent the broadcast media affect people's attitudes and beliefs, but there is no doubt that they could very easily subvert the processes of democratic debate in favour of political parties who gain control over editorial content. Democratic freedom depends on the separation of broadcasting from the state.

This leaves us with something of a puzzle: the government of the day cannot set BBC policy, and yet as a public institution, the BBC cannot simply make its own mind up about what it is in the business of doing. We have already outlined in some depth why 'market accountability' is not an option, since this can result in outcomes which do not always match people's needs.

An alternative, implied by some of the BBC's literature, is that the licence fee already operates as form of direct accountability between the BBC's audiences and the broadcaster:

> [The licence fee] establishes the broadcaster's direct duty to serve every household and meet all the diversity and range of interests that involves. (*The BBC Beyond 2000*, p 20)

This certainly establishes a direct link between what television owners pay for and what the BBC receives. Unlike other public services, the BBC's revenue is not distributed from a general taxation 'pot' after inter-departmental wrangling, but is determined by the level of the licence fee – decided in advance – and the number of licence payers. Thus, it is certainly true that those who pay have a clear idea of how much they as individuals contribute, in relation to what they get by way of a service. For other public services, the contribution of a single household to any individual area of welfare is obscured by the general nature of the tax revenue raised and distributed by the Treasury.

There is thus somewhat greater accountability in the sense that the 'tax' payer for broadcasting has greater information about what they are getting for their money. But they cannot exercise formal control – the crucial element of accountability – to any greater degree than the general taxpayers and users of public services. Payment is compulsory, and the BBC is not obliged to answer directly to the viewer. Formal accountability to the service user – as in other services – is mediated by representative institutions – inevitably so if the BBC is to do more than simply respond as a market competitor would.

This does not mean that the BBC is able to ignore what the licence fee payer says or does – if enough people switch off then this will have consequences. Further, the existence of a direct 'fee' may encourage consumers of BBC services to be especially vigilant in holding the programme makers to account – more so, for example, than if funding were organised through a hypothecated tax which only obliged contributions from a section of the community. And better to understand what they want or need, the BBC engages in numerous outreach exercises, such as the 'BBC Listens' which encourages wider and deeper debate through public meetings, focus groups, seminars, on air discussions and online. These strategies of engaging in a more sophisticated way with the audience enhance accountability in the sense that the BBC becomes more accessible and open to the public, and more receptive to its views. But formally and legally, accountability 'follows the money' and that, for public institutions, means upwards to ministers – in the BBC's case, as representatives of the Crown.

So what version of formal accountability can balance political independence with social obligations? The compromise reached is that of a public corporation operating under Royal Charter, independently controlled by a board or Governors, and following objectives codified in an Agreement between the BBC and the Secretary of State, both renegotiable intermittently. The relevant portion of the Agreement that comes closest to defining public purpose was outlined above. We believe that some form of accountability mechanism of this kind must exist, and is the proper focus of improving the way in which the BBC pursues CORA-type objectives.

It is clear that much of this already matches CORA objectives. If accountability to its licence payers is to be improved in the context of achieving these objectives, then one possibility is that they are specified in more detail. Could reference be made, not just to the type of programmes which should be produced, but to the social ends which are being pursued? The following are possibilities: a requirement to make innovative programmes as a means of widening social opportunities; to cater for the widest range of interests and particularly those who might otherwise be excluded from national life; or to place special emphasis on national events where the nation can 'come together' but without offending international co-operation. The template is already there – for example, specific requirements are made to provide educational programming and impartial news.

These suggestions may appear contentious. There is a perpetual danger of any broadcaster becoming too closely associated with the political agenda of the day. The public purposes of the BBC must never simply amount to a Party Manifesto. However, there is no clear division between public purposes, even where they appear to command consensus, and government policy. Even apparently uncontroversial objectives which accord with the perceived values of the age will have their passionate opponents. Is it not possible, therefore, to set out in greater detail the BBC's public purposes, both to enable those who oppose them to engage in honest and open debate, and to provide a clear standard against which the BBC's output can be assessed?

6.3 Pursuing CORA in a multichannel era

One apparent paradox for the public sector broadcaster is that although they should not be driven by ratings, they nonetheless wish as many people to watch their programmes as possible. The higher the ratings the better – unless this is achieved by simply aiming to maximise the numbers watching!

It is, of course, more complex than this. As we have seen, widening opportunities through programming for minorities can be achieved with small audiences: whether for a rare opera or an Asian comedy show. Similarly, an in–depth piece of analysis which uncovers flaws in the working of government policy may also obtain low ratings, but it is justified if it succeeds in policy changes which benefit us all – including those who do not watch.

On the other hand, the success of public purposes which emphasise national cohesion, the provision of general information or the introduction of innovative programming, tend to be measured ultimately by the numbers watching. After all, it is no good claiming a new drama serial is 'daring and original' if only a handful of viewers watch it. Innovation does not imply quality. The 'opportunity' objective is about giving people what they want and need but are unable properly to articulate in a market environment, either because they do not know their own tastes or because they tend to be short-sighted about what is in their best interests.

The trick, then, in achieving CORA ends partly depends on encouraging people to watch what they might not demand from a private market. The BBC's strategy for achieving this has in the past depended on mixing the more straightforward type of programming also offered by its commercial rivals with those programmes serving public purposes. This is a sensible strategy – the potential BBC audience must feel that as a broadcaster it has relevance to their immediate wants if they are also to try new, difficult or more serious programmes. Not only is this a sensible strategy but it has largely been successful, at least as indicated by audience 'reach' figures. According to the BBC itself (1997) 'in 95 per cent of UK households last year someone viewed or listened to at least two hours of BBC programming a week'. By nurturing this relevance to the whole community, rather less obviously commercial prospects such as David Attenborough's *Life* natural history series, the Monty Python comedy films and *Pride and Prejudice* all enjoy mass audiences.

But the commercial environment is changing. The BBC faces greater competition now than it ever has before. The introduction of Channel 4 and

Channel 5 in the eighties and nineties added to ITV in the free-to-air market, which is now supplemented by a significant pay-TV sector consisting of BSkyB and a host of smaller broadcasters providing niche channels on cable and satellite. Local radio has similarly expanded in the commercial sector, with 10 commercial stations available to the average listener in 1997. Digital television will increase this competition, with free-to-air DTT adding ITV2 and a new Channel 4 film channel to literally hundreds of new cable and satellite pay channels. The total share of BBC viewing has dropped from 43 per cent in 1992, to 41 per cent in 1998, and is widely accepted as likely to fall further. Furthermore, the number of very large audiences – for example, those over 10 million, has dropped significantly between 1992 and 1997.[3]

This commercial competition has a potentially more serious impact on the BBC and its ability to achieve its public purposes than that experienced by other public welfare services. Compare the position of health and education. These central institutions of the welfare state also have public purposes: to provide high quality health care and education to everyone equally, whilst at the same time ensuring that the nation's resources are not wasted on ineffective or inappropriate services. As in the broadcast field, private provision has never been outlawed, leaving the public purposes less than totally fulfilled. Some people choose to pay privately in order to receive a higher standard of health or education. Such are the compromises of a 'free' society.

But the NHS and state secondary education have one powerful advantage over their commercial rivals: they are free. Their public objectives can be obtained, without coercion, by subsidy, such that the vast majority of people choose of their own accord to join the public sector because it makes personal financial sense to do so. The BBC, on the other hand, faces three 'free' commercial rivals thanks to the peculiarities of advertising based funding. Of course, these are indirectly paid for by the viewer, but they remain free-at-the-point-of-use. Even the pay channels do not charge prices to compare with the equivalent private market in health and education – moreover the benefit is immediate and pleasurable, rather than deferred and, in the case of health, distressing.

The BBC will thus need to work harder in the future to retain a critical mass of viewers. The key variable may be, not the proportion of overall viewing (which almost certainly continue to fall), but 'reach'. This variable measures what proportion of people turn to the BBC for at least some proportion of their viewing week. Thus in a sense it is a measure of 'relevance'. But in order to retain this relevance, and thus its ability to deliver on CORA objectives, it will paradoxically need to become even more expert at competing directly for ratings. It will compete, not to maximise the value of advertising time or the number of subscriptions, but in order to encourage viewers to join the BBC and stumble across or sample programming they otherwise might not.

Competing for ratings in this way may also need to be more evenly spread across the network. Currently, BBC One contributes most to this task, but in order to maximise the public purpose of BBC Two consideration should be given to encouraging more people to think that this is a channel 'for them' – at least some of the time. Similar issues arise with reference to radio. Recent accusations that Radios 3 and 4 have 'dumbed down' are misguided on this analysis – these stations should continue to develop programming which can attract a wider audience while retaining their traditional programme focus. Serving minority communities should not extend to protecting whole channels or stations for particular segments of society.[4]

7 Conclusion

We have discussed how broadcasting is a potentially powerful technology for promoting CORA ends, and why they require a publicly financed broadcaster such as the BBC to ensure their full potential. Further, we have suggested that many of the stated aims of the BBC match up well to CORA.

We have also noted there are difficulties in pursuing public purposes related to CORA. The principles could be interpreted in ways which are inimical to the good of society – particularly 'community'. And public purposes are liable to shift over time: CORA may go out of political fashion.

This also raises the question of accountability. Formally, the expenditure of public money must be accounted for by elected representatives; at the same time, the BBC needs to keep its distance from political influence. One possibility is for the Agreement to be specified in terms more closely related to 'purpose' as well as programme type. This would allow for the occasional renegotiation of what that purpose is, while simultaneously avoiding the danger of continual political interference.

But for now we believe CORA principles chime well with the existing stated purposes of the BBC. If it is to continue to achieve them it may have to become more adept at securing audiences, given the inevitable growth in the number of its competitors. Otherwise its ability to provide opportunities and services to all communities will be weakened. CORA and the BBC may not be a marriage made in heaven, but it is more than simply a marriage of convenience.

References

BBC (1998) *The BBC Beyond 2000*, BBC, London.
BBC (1997) *Governing the BBC: Broadcasting, the public interest and accountability*, BBC, London.
Etzioni, A. (1993) *The Spirit of Community: the Re-invention of American Society*. New York: Touchstone.
Kumar, K. (1986), 'Public service broadcasting and the public interest', in MacCabe, C and Stewart, O (eds) *The BBC and Public Service Broadcasting*, Manchester University Press, Manchester.

Le Grand, J. (1998) 'The third way begins with CORA' *The New Statesman*, 6 March, 26-27.

Notes

1   We would like to thank Patricia Hodgson (Director of Policy and Planning), Simon Milner (Senior Advisor, Policy Development), Dominic Morris (Controller of Policy Development), Ed Richards (Controller of Corporate Strategy), Richard Sambrook (Head of Newsgathering, BBC News) and Will Wyatt (Chief Executive, BBC Broadcast) for giving up their time to discuss these issues with us. The views expressed, however, remain ours alone.

2   It should also be noted, however, that some reporting of the riots was restricted in order to discourage 'copycat' rioting - in other words to discourage irresponsible behaviour. This is relevant to the discussion of 'responsibility'.

3   Unpublished BBC research. See chapter 1 in this volume.

4   Radios 3 and 4 are predominantly listened to by 'better off' groups according to BBC analysis; BBC Two is also favoured by the better off, although the difference is much less marked.

Chapter 6

Broadcasting and the Socially Excluded

Ian Corfield

This chapter addresses the question 'how does and should broadcasting and particularly the BBC serve the socially excluded?'.

Social exclusion is rightly regarded as a significant blight on our modern society at the turn of a new millennium - on the individual people affected by it, their families and communities. Free-to-air broadcasting has always been seen as one way in which everyone is connected to the world around them. In the age of digital television, the Internet and a largely commercial broadcasting market, it is important to consider to what extent broadcasting will continue to serve the socially excluded. Given the broad public obligations required of the BBC, its particular role in serving the socially excluded could be crucial. These issues are addressed in this chapter in three main sections:

- An examination of the salient features of social exclusion today, its causes and how it might develop over the next 10 years.

- An assessment of the current role of broadcasting in general and the BBC in particular in serving the socially excluded.

- An analysis of how new communications technology and the move towards an information society might change the way the BBC serves the socially excluded.

1 The Salient Features of Social Exclusion

Poverty and social exclusion are often seen as synonymous by politicians and in the Press. They are clearly closely related. Many socially excluded people are evidently in poverty, on whatever measure. But many people in relative poverty are probably not socially excluded. It is worth unpicking this relationship further before assessing how social exclusion might develop in the future. Despite the caveats, an understanding of the current state of poverty in Britain is a sensible starting point for examining social exclusion.

1.1 Poverty

Poverty is hardly a new phenomenon. Social reformers throughout the century have sought measures to eradicate it. However, in 1998 poverty is still a social and political issue.

Measures of absolute poverty are open to wide interpretation. The indicators used to assess people's lifestyles have by necessity changed over time. However, it is difficult to avoid the conclusion that as the standard of living of the population has improved, some of this has been reflected in better conditions for the worst off.

Relative poverty is different. Research shows a widening of income divisions across society. Britain is reported to have seen the biggest growth in inequality of any country other than New Zealand. The percentage of households below average income[1] (the most frequently used definition of poverty) rose from 9 per cent in 1979 to 24 per cent in 1992, leaving the bottom 10 per cent of households with 2.5 per cent of total income.[2] In 1997 one in three children were reported in be living in households earning below half of average income - three times the level in 1979.[3]

1.2 Social exclusion

Although social exclusion is largely connected with poverty, it is over simplistic to equate the two. Social exclusion is more widely defined than poverty, by a set of non-material as well as material factors. There are a legion of definitions. Here are four:

- The government's Social Exclusion Unit describe social exclusion as 'what can happen when individuals or areas suffer from a combination of linked problems such as unemployment, poor skills, low incomes, poor housing, high crime environments, bad health and family breakdown.'[4]

- The Institute for Public Policy Research have emphasised how social exclusion relates not just to income but to a set of self re-enforcing divisions within society. Not all of those in poverty should be regarded as socially excluded (see Figure 6.1).

- Perri 6, of the think-tank Demos, has argued that social exclusion is related to the networks people operate within. He describes how most people have strong (family and neighbours) and weak (acquaintances and work contacts) networks.[5] Although many of the worst off have strong networks they lack the weak ones that are needed for advancement. Those described as 'socially excluded' might be seen to lack regular access to both types of network.

- Tony Atkinson argues that social exclusion is about a lack of 'agency'[6] or freedom in exercising important choices in life. Poverty may be the main factor in loss of agency but discrimination, ageing or lack of access to information can also contribute.

Although more precise definitions and evidence on the scale of social exclusion are not yet common currency; different groups in society today

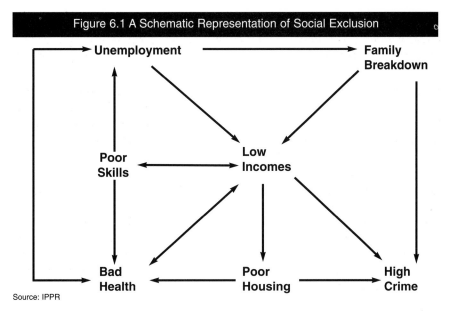

Figure 6.1 A Schematic Representation of Social Exclusion

Source: IPPR

appear to lead evermore divergent lifestyles. In particular, the quality of education, health, the local environment and relations to the democratic process can be demonstrably different across society.

The trend towards those at the bottom being least likely to vote or play an active part in politics[7] appears to be relatively recent. More established are the trends towards those at the top of society being less likely to truant,[8] more likely to achieve good grades and attend the best universities.[9] Equally, those at the bottom have very often been more likely to have a poor diet, often living in 'food deserts',[10] are less likely to live beyond the average age[11] and are ill more often.[12]

Social divisions combined with the growth of relative poverty seem to have hit certain groups of people hardest. Current evidence suggests that four groups are most badly affected:[13]

- *Poor pensioners*. As the population ages a sharp divide appears to be emerging between affluent pensioners (predominantly those with a second pension) and a large group in relative poverty (mainly on the state pension). This division is likely to widen.[14]

- *Single parents*. Single parents are more likely than dual parent households to become socially excluded. They are more likely to be affected by a vicious circle of inadequate childcare, a subsequent inability to take up work opportunities and a distancing from the wider community. Many find themselves in poverty.[15]

- *Unemployed men*. Male employment has dipped in almost exact proportion to the growth in female employment[16] and men in general find it particularly difficult to cope with inactivity. Older unemployed men are often on incapacity benefit and live in some of the most depressed areas of the country. They often find inactivity socially debilitating. Young men find it more difficult then their female peers to break out of unemployment.[17] They often are involved in or are blamed for street crime, are least active in the pursuit of work and are less likely to move into full time education.[18]

- *Some ethnic minorities.* Either because of poverty or discrimination, some ethnic minorities are ghettoised in housing and employment terms. This particularly affects the Afro-Caribbean community; who on average earn around 82 per cent of the median white wage, are less likely to be in managerial work and have the highest level of comparative unemployment.[19] Although most second and third generation Indians are increasingly integrated fully into society, evidence suggests that the many in Pakistani and Bangladeshi communities remain excluded.[20]

1.3 How social exclusion might develop over the next decade

Government intervention could stall or reverse the growth of relative poverty and social exclusion. The recently established Social Exclusion Unit is focusing its efforts on a series of specific areas,[21] including truancy, homelessness and the worst housing estates. They prescribe 'joined-up-government' working with other organisations to relieve the problem.

However, if current trends prove hard to reverse, we are likely to see three particular developments over the next ten years:

- *Entrenchment of a 30:40:30 society.*[22] We may see reinforcement of the trend towards what Will Hutton identified as a 30:40:30 society. Hutton argued that social and income divisions were leading to a situation where two thirds of people live in relative comfort, whilst one third are in relative poverty (the bottom 30). Within the better off, a majority feel insecure about their future prospects because of flexible working arrangements (the middle 40). The exact proportions are unclear (it might be 80-20), but the trend is becoming clearer. Pensioners, single parents, the unemployed and ethnic minorities are likely to dominate the group of the worst off.

- *Increasing division between the information haves and have-nots.* Many activities are likely to become more difficult without access to information technology and an understanding of how to use it: using government services, gaining access to banks; and making use of educational opportunities. Competitive pressures and technological advance may reduce the price of basic IT equipment over time, but the affluent in society are always likely to remain well ahead in their understanding and access to advanced technology.[23]

- *Increasing problems associated with an aging society.* Age is one of the greatest contributors to social exclusion. Britain is getting older as healthier lifestyles and modern medicine combine with reductions in the birth rate to give us a far higher dependency ratio.[24] As well as income divisions among the elderly, discrimination against them as a group could grow. The strength of the 'grey pound'[25] and the political power of such a significant minority mean they are unlikely to be ignored. However, in a society where respect for the elderly is declining, the rights of this group could come under pressure.

This brief overview of social trends demonstrates that the UK has experienced growing relative poverty and apparently greater social divisions. Unless government action has a significant effect it is likely that these trends will worsen. Social exclusion will rise rather than fall.

2 How Broadcasting Serves the Socially Excluded

It would be wrong to proceed on the assumption that the BBC has a monopoly among broadcasters in serving the socially excluded. Commercial broadcasters can help to build a more inclusive society. Self-interest, enlightened or otherwise, means certain commercial broadcasters also serve the socially excluded since they are a group of interest to some advertisers. Also, although regulated differently to the BBC, commercial terrestrial broadcasters are subject to certain public obligations, requiring them to recognise the demands of the socially excluded.

Thus the BBC is not alone in providing services for the socially excluded. ITV remains a highly popular universal service provider. In the near future it is unlikely that a splintering of the ITV network would leave the BBC as a lone universal provider of well-funded popular programmes.

Internal BBC research shows that the Top 20 programmes popular with people in socially excluded groups are split relatively evenly between the BBC and ITV. That said, the top ten shows with the highest percentage of socially excluded viewers are all on ITV. Through programmes like *Coronation Street* ITV has as much potential as the BBC to create the common reference points that can generate inclusion. Equally, as we move into the multi-channel digital age it is possible that BskyB and cable providers might begin to produce more services targeted at the socially excluded.

That said, there is a widespread expectation that the BBC, as the UK's primary public service broadcaster, should take a lead in serving the socially excluded. This section attempts to identify where the BBC's strengths and weaknesses lie and reviews how its activities might be improved.

2.1 Providing a universal service that generates a sense of inclusion

Very few people are directly excluded from the BBC's service. 99 per cent of the UK population can receive terrestrial television and radio services.[26] Britain has the third highest television ownership in the world (after USA

& Bermuda),[27] and UK adults watch an average of two and a half-hours of television a day.[28]

Among the 'socially excluded' usage is even higher. Those not in work watch on average 1 hour more television per day than those in work.[29] The BBC's audience share among some sections of the socially excluded is considerably higher than its share across all audiences.[30]

The BBC also has some advantages over other universal service providers. It is the only broadcaster operating across all media (television, radio, and the Internet) that can co-ordinate its activities in these media. It has also maintained audience share far better than ITV in the face of competition.[31]

Yet, as the BBC faces the most intense competition in its history, the key issue is whether it can differentiate itself from other providers. In particular, how can the BBC develop as the broadcaster serving the whole audience and in the process create a greater sense of inclusion?

- *By reflecting a genuine understanding of the audience in what the BBC does.* The BBC's audience awareness work appears to be among the most advanced in this field. However, as the '100 Faces of Britain' work (a sophisticated audience segmentation exercise) revealed, the BBC probably still has an imperfect understanding of the issues that concern the socially excluded and so cannot fully meet their needs.

  In particular as producers are likely to continue to be of a different background to such audiences, a more 'audience driven' culture will probably be important. In a media environment where success is so often based on total viewing figures this is more easily said than done. But it is certainly important to ensure that insights concerning all elements of the audience inform scheduling and other programme decisions.

  As a public service broadcaster the BBC has a responsibility to seek and take account of the views of the wider public. Audiences, however, are often sceptical of consultation exercises and the BBC may need to review its processes to ensure the best possible response. In particular, the BBC should examine the participation of the socially excluded in its consultation exercises.

  Consultation exercises can also ensure that programmes and services better reflects the demands of the whole community.[32] The BBC has run some successful consultation exercises; for example BBC Online generated 1,600 responses.[33] However, the rolling programme of consultation *The BBC Listens*, designed to inform the Governors, should be broadened to inform service decisions among programme makers, commissioners and schedulers. This might mean adopting a more accessible and user friendly approach to consultation among all social groups than has been used to date.

- *Producing popular output that reflects the needs and aspirations of the socially excluded.* It is tempting to argue that the BBC should produce programmes deliberately targeted at the socially excluded. Meeting the needs of specific audiences, however, is probably not best done by categorising particular programmes for particular people.[34] The results can sometimes be mediocre and watched by only a minority of the target audience.

In particular, the socially excluded may not be best served by producing specific programmes for them. Instead, existing popular and special interest programmes are most likely to reflect their needs and aspirations. For example, the worst off probably want to watch holiday programming that includes vacations they can afford and others they can only dream of. Young unemployed men may enjoy programming about cars and car maintenance but are unlikely to switch on for 'Car Maintenance For The Unemployed'.

This does not preclude dedicated programmes for minorities being shown or occasionally enjoying a peak viewing slot. However, it does imply that 'deficit' programming, made without evidence of community demand, is unlikely to be a sustainable strategy.

- *Developing a common 'stock of knowledge' for the whole community.* The BBC is most likely to aid social inclusion by creating a set of common references points that everyone can understand. This can range from making news accessible, to producing popular classic drama (12 million watched *Pride and Prejudice*) through to making children's programming the talk of the playground or the World Cup open to all. The BBC already goes a long way towards creating what Andrew Graham calls a stock of 'common knowledge'.[35]

In practice this might be taken even further by shifting resources into highly popular quality programming areas like Radio 1, Radio 5 Live and sports programming. Providing programmes are broadly of good quality or innovative, the BBC should be robust in legitimating this strategy with pressure groups and parliamentarians who accuse it of dumbing down.

2.2 Having a brand that people value and trust

Surveys demonstrate that the BBC is a strong brand[36] - both recognised and valued by the great majority of the UK population, and by many millions across the world. It is also seen as a symbol of quality that embodies a set of values,[37] signifying the trust viewers, citizens, and parents put in it. As a brand it plays a significant part in people's lives.

Of course there are many other strong brands that also have values. *Coca-Cola* looks to define the brand as individualistic, *Sainsbury's* as family based and *Levi's* for the rebel. The BBC brand can be important for the socially excluded because they receive something that is seen as a symbol of quality by everyone. Other brands can exclude people through image or price. In building its brand the BBC has the opportunity to generate a greater sense of inclusion.

The BBC probably still has some way to go in persuading the whole audience that its brand embodies all of their values. For example in news, although the BBC is seen as accurate and professional, it loses out to commercial broadcasters on being either entertaining or engaging. Young people in particular are less loyal to BBC News than to news provided by commercial broadcasters.[38]

The need for continued vigilance over brand strength is underlined by competitive pressures. BSkyB is thought to be spending £60m this year promoting digital television and developing a more 'friendly provider' rather than 'commercial giant' image. Competitors are likely to seek different images to the BBC. Yet at the same time some will probably align themselves with BBC values. In this environment sustaining and building its brand values among all sections of the population should be a priority of increasing importance to the BBC.

2.3 Offering value for money and an appropriate funding regime

The way an organisation is funded is likely to affect who it thinks its audiences are and how it serves them. In the digital age, with masses of channels to choose from, the licence fee is likely to become more of a focus for debate. This is reflected in the terms of the reference for the review of the licence fee in 1999. Although the Secretary of State, Chris Smith, stated clearly that the position of the licence fee was not under threat in the medium-term, its long-term sustainability would be considered.

In this context. it is worth considering whether, in serving the socially excluded, the fee is a benefit or a hindrance.

Although debate rages about how the licence fee is spent, most objective measures indicate that it provides value for money. Looked at as a percentage of leisure spend,[39] in comparison to the number of hours watched[40] and compared with other countries,[41] the licence fee looks a good deal. Debate has tended to focus not on cutting the fee but on whether it should be supplemented by other forms of income.[42]

In relation to the socially excluded, two points are commonly made in favour of the licence fee as a funding mechanism. First is that it connects the BBC with all of the audience because it is a direct payment. Second is that everyone benefits, and as such the worst off have access to a service they could not otherwise afford – a collective good. As with hospitals, schools and the police, the BBC has an obligation to deliver a service for all irrespective of their income or status.

However, as a compulsory levy the licence fee is controversial. It might be argued that other systems retaining the main benefits of the licence fee for the socially excluded whilst reducing the direct cost could be designed. For example, if the concern is with maintaining a link to viewers whilst funding a collective good then an argument might be put for having the BBC funded 50 per cent by the licence fee and 50 per cent by general taxation. Appropriate regulation might make such a system, at least superficially, very similar to the current position.

Such schemes are in fact likely to generate as many problems as they solve – raising concern for instance about the BBC's independence from Government. That said, the BBC should probably concentrate less on justifying the licence fee as its funding mechanism and more on the public need for public service broadcasting. The BBC is a force to educate, entertain and inform – an agent of social change. The BBC serves all sections of society because its staff and audiences regard it as a service to the nation, not just to individual licence fee payers.

In the medium term, the licence fee's future is secured, but the 1999 Review will examine the prospect for changes in the concessions regime. There is likely to be considerable public pressure for new concessions specifically directed at low-income groups, for example pensioners on social security. This would be of direct financial benefit to a group of the worst off.

In public policy terms, however, the benefits may be superficial. It is debatable how much the government or the socially excluded, beyond the direct beneficiaries, would gain.

Firstly, this would effectively be an increase in social security benefit paid for by a cut in the BBC's revenues or an increase in the standard licence fee for remaining households. Using the BBC or other organisations in this way might subvert their funding systems. It can also be seen as robbing Peter to pay Paul. Additional benefits, should they be necessary, are probably best paid directly through the Exchequer, as they are for example with winter fuel payments for pensioners.

Secondly, a view could be taken either that the BBC is over-funded or that the licence fee should be progressive. However, whatever the merit or otherwise of these views, they are separate from arguments in favour of any particular concession. They should probably be seen as such.

Finally, whilst BBC services may well survive an initial cut, over time they may be damaged. Although reducing Licence fees for the worst off may have merit, there appears to be little logic behind putting one deserving group in front of another – especially at the expense of service levels for all.

The practicalities, as well as the principles, of the licence fee system are also a point of discussion. The current concessions can appear ill conceived, non-payment remains an issue and payment methods, though improved, could still present a barrier to the worst off.

The 1999 Review will consider changing some aspects of the concessionary system. There are two concessions of particular interest – the blind concession, set over 30 years ago, giving either £1.25 off the fee or exemption for a sound-only television receiver, and the ARC (Accommodation for

Residential Care) concession giving substantial reductions to people in certain types of residential or sheltered accommodation for the elderly or disabled. The take up of blind concessions is minimal and the perceived inequity of ARC increases, as the make up of people in relevant accommodation becomes less uniform[43] and some lose out.

These concessions can make the BBC appear petty (although the BBC does not determine the concessions). They are the basis of numerous complaints and questions in Parliament. The BBC reaction to this scrutiny can, from the outside, look defensive and unnecessarily fearful of the wider concessions debate.

The BBC should probably be open-minded about a review of the system. Considerably more generous concessions for the blind need not be prohibitively costly and would probably be popular. A re-assessment of the 1986 Peacock Report claim that ARC costs more to collect than it raises[44] could then take place. If it remains true, the criteria could be widened to reduce complaints and the charges abolished. Alternatively, merging the ARC concession with the concession for hotels[45] – including more homes in the process – might be a better option.

These changes are not completely consistent but do have a rationale behind them – reducing collection costs and complaints – and could produce a more practical system. More importantly they should allow the BBC to focus on the real issues around avoidance and payment methods.

The BBC has had considerable success in reducing evasion since taking over collection from the Home Office in 1991. There are currently 6 per cent of households with televisions who do not pay their licence fee.[46]

However, licence fee collection is expensive, it costs the BBC £109m[47] per year and tracking the last group of non-payers could add to that bill. A significant percentage of these non-payers are in the poorest areas in Britain and likely to be unemployed or low paid.[48] Collection from these people might bring negative publicity and political criticism.

The BBC is concerned over the costs and problems associated with non-payment. The use of fines and, at the last resort, prison as a sanction is obviously only effective against those who won't (rather than can't) pay and even then prison can be seen as a draconian deterrent. Instead the BBC should look again at its portfolio of payment methods to help those who have genuine problems in paying the fee.

Although the Licence fee can now be paid for in a variety of ways some of the options are only open to fee payers who fall into certain categories. 'Cash-Easy-Entry', for example, is only open to those in hardship without a bank account. Such systems are limited in their effectiveness because fee payers already have serious payment problems before they can opt for easier schemes.

Some further research into payment methods, looking at UK and international best practice, might highlight possible options. Other organisations such as utilities and building societies operate a range of payment options open to everyone. Some of these could be adapted to the licence fee.

2.4 *Running effective educational campaigns*

The BBC's core mission - to educate, entertain and inform - is often best demonstrated by its educational programming and campaigns. Recent successes in the areas of computer literacy, cancer and relationships have attracted significant attention from the public and the wider education world.[49]

Equally, on-going initiatives on crime, literacy & numeracy make a significant addition to the BBC's community involvement. Significant numbers of the least well off in society value these various initiatives. For example, 16 per cent of people ringing into the 'Computers don't Bite' campaign were unemployed.[50]

Recognition of the role the BBC is able to play can be seen from the numerous partnerships between the BBC and educational organisations, including relevant Government departments. The BBC's relationship with the Open University is the most long-standing of these partnerships. It also works with the National Extension College, the Basic Skills Agency and the Libraries Association on particular programmes, campaigns or initiatives. A major plank of BBC Education's strategy for maximising its effectiveness is using these partnerships to put individuals in touch with more specialist learning providers.

The BBC does not claim to be unique in providing educational programming generally or for the socially excluded specifically. Channel 4 Education and Granada, to name but two, have significant operations and as the education market grows the BBC is likely to face more competitors.

In this competitive market the BBC should be focusing on its strengths. First, it is the only broadcaster currently able to run educational programming across all formats (television, radio and the Internet). Secondly, it is one of the only providers committed to meeting the educational requirements of the least well off.

It is a little difficult to see the BBC being able to capitalise on these strengths unless education is a core BBC activity. Steps have been taken to integrate education into wider programming and BBC Education now focuses on the education needs of the country as a whole. But more might be done to repeat the success of initiatives like 'Computers don't bite' and to bring a wider range of learning opportunities to people stimulated by such BBC campaigns.

The BBC should also continue building partnerships that ensure a high quality of treatment for people when BBC campaigns via call-ins or the Internet lead them to contact other organisations. Clear scheduling priorities could focus BBC resources on a few key campaigns, as

'Computers Don't Bite' did. A commitment might be given to maintain the current number of hours for specifically educational programming. And running more programming of this type in daytime hours might better ensure access for the target audience.

2.5 So how well is the BBC serving the socially excluded?

This quick overview suggests that the BBC is making a positive contribution to serving the socially excluded in four areas – providing an inclusive universal service, building a brand that people value and trust, offering value for money and running effective educational campaigns.

However, it is also clear that the BBC is not unique in offering broadcast services for the socially excluded. It is apparent that in areas where competition is increasing the BBC is rightly keen to improve its performance.

So far much of the discussion could be regarded as focusing on the analogue environment. To complete this review of the BBC's role it is necessary to look forward to the implications of the digital age. The next section will assess the opportunities and threats presented by technological developments.

3 Serving the Socially Excluded in the Digital Age

The digital age will see a significant shake up in broadcasting; for the BBC, its commercial competitors and audiences. The convergence of communications is likely to mean that the relationship between television and the Internet will become more important. Digital delivers not only the possibility of hundreds of television and radio channels but also interactivity with individual audience members via computer applications in set-top boxes and integrated digital televisions.

For the socially excluded, there is the danger that digital could enhance exclusion by limiting access to programmes previously available on free-to-air networks. Moreover, it is likely that cost of consumer equipment and access charges will limit widespread take-up of the Internet, via PC or digital television, in the near future.[51]

The BBC could help to promote an inclusive digital age by ensuring the 'digital dividend'[52] it has promised to audiences applies equally to the socially excluded. This might involve reaching out beyond straightforward programming to intervene in the way the digital age develops. The BBC should act as a latter day 'Nation's champion' and in the process help British broadcasting more generally.

No one really knows what the digital age will be like. The BBC helped invent broadcasting and should seek to have a similar influence in the development of digital. It should develop a vision of what the digital age might look like going far beyond how it will affect the BBC. Then, rather than simply defend the decision to launch digital services, the BBC should show confidence in its own convictions and robustly promote a wider vision.

In particular there are three areas where the BBC should act as the Nation's champion', promote its vision of digital and support the socially excluded. It should go into battle to secure access for all. It should help make quality digital content a reality. Finally, it should build the BBC digital brand as a trusted friend.

3.1 Battling to secure access for all in a new technological environment

The digital age presents at least two technological stumbling blocks for the socially excluded. The first is the straightforward problem of access to consumer equipment. Over time, technologically developments and market competition are likely to reduce the price of basic digital receivers to a level where nearly everyone can afford them. However, at least initially, the worst off in society will be directly excluded from the digital age by cost barriers.

Second, there is the more complex issue of divisions between digital consumers. It is likely that the audience will divide between the 'interactive' and the 'passive' depending on their access to and understanding of new technology. Passive consumers will simply receive the new channels. Interactive viewers will be able to react either through the television or Internet to what is going on in front of them. Those with interactive capacity will get a very different experience.

Yet there is nothing about the new digital receivers that necessarily means an end to free-to-air, universal services. Although the BBC cannot intervene directly in these hardware and software issues, it could seek to protect the interests of Licence fee payers. The BBC should take a stance on some of key issues around inclusion and access.

This is likely to mean the BBC becoming the 'people's voice' in the political battle over access. As an organisation working with all the major gateway providers it should argue passionately in favour of the consumer, and particularly those consumers with little or no spending power.

Securing free-to-air carriage of BBC services on all three digital platforms must remain a crucial BBC objective. Over the longer term as the market grows, it will also be important for the socially excluded that the BBC continues to seek alliances that enable all viewers to access all BBC services. Initiatives such as putting kiosks with access to BBC Online in libraries (a scheme run jointly with the Libraries Association) will continue to be vital.

However, concerns may be raised about the BBC's involvement in subscription services. At present these are restricted to repeating programming already seen on free to air channels and so have few implications for inclusion. Maintaining this principle in partnerships, such as that developed with Flextech, will be important if the BBC is not to contribute to exclusion.

The BBC should take a particular public interest in how access for the socially excluded might best be maintained after analogue transmissions are switched off. The government will announce in the next two years its plans for the current analogue signal on which all terrestrial television is transmitted. The way this is handled could have serious implications for the socially excluded.

Analogue 'switch-off' could mean universal television is no longer available to those without digital receivers. In addition the software in receivers might be used to block freely available programming. In the worst case scenario, switch-off could mean a significant number of the worst off having no broadcasting service.

One suggested solution, from the Institute for Public Policy Research is the 'Switch-Off Fund'. They propose that the significant sums which could be raised by auctioning off the analogue spectrum in advance of switch-off, are used to extend digital access either by subsidising signal roll out to remote areas or by paying for or subsidising set top boxes for needy groups.[53]

There are two main problems with such a scheme. First, it could at the margin create a further extension of the 'poverty trap' for those on benefit – as the prospect of a free television adds to the opportunity cost of taking work. Second, news of the idea may result in millions not buying into digital in the hope of securing a free set or money off. Either result makes the chances of such schemes passing Treasury scrutiny unlikely but should not prevent the BBC considering the issue seriously.

3.2 Making quality digital content a reality

Access is an important issue but so too is ensuring that the digital age is not simply about more channels and more Internet sites. Ensuring the availability of high quality content is another way the BBC serves the socially excluded. As the digital age develops this might become more important in maintaining the 'common stock of knowledge' discussed earlier.

Innovation is probably the best way to avoid a 'more channels – less choice' scenario. The full depth of BBC resources, working closely with other players, might be required to achieve a different outcome. It will however be a missed opportunity if the digital environment is channels similar to those already available on cable and satellite but delivered by a new technology.

The advent of digital will probably pose some tough choices. On the one hand, it is difficult to see the BBC matching the range of output offered by thousands of channels. On the other hand the BBC should continue serving a range of different groups.

In particular, the BBC should continue to run programming of value to increasingly unfashionable groups like pensioners and the bottom third of society. The worsening social trends described above are likely to emphasise the BBC's unique position in providing programming for these groups. However, the BBC would seek to do so without becoming the 'broadcaster of last resort'.

The BBC is probably best placed to occupy the centre-stage in producing high-quality content for the digital age. It should pursue a popular programming strategy that allows diversity but does not seek to replicate the range of digital offerings. As with its analogue strategy, the BBC will best serve the socially excluded by providing popular programmes that reflect their needs and opportunities.

3.3 Building the BBC brand as a trusted friend

Championing access and delivering high quality content free-to-air is likely to help the BBC brand. As other players attempt to identify themselves with a similar set of values to the BBC, an enhanced role in the digital age should put the BBC one step ahead of the game.

However, as well as being a 'champion' the BBC could also act as a 'friend'. Ensuring people are neither exploited nor excluded in the digital age is a role the BBC could play. At the same time it would underline their positioning as 'trusted guide'.[54] Two areas are particularly key – developing a guide to the digital age and expanding educational programming.

The prospective death of the general channel due to the rise of niche channels and the Internet has probably been exaggerated. Viewers already surf channels looking for particular interests or programming. It will soon be technically possible to programme your television to do the searching for you automatically. Your personal selection of content could then be available for viewing at your leisure. But this scenario, often referred to as the 'Daily Me',[55] may not appeal to many people. Editors and schedulers are likely to continue to have jobs. Viewers will look to channels like BBC One and ITV to offer a range of enjoyable and stimulating programmes.

However, people are likely to require a guide around the maze-like world of digital television. The BBC, either through an online service or via television and radio, could be that unbiased facilitator – guiding people around the new age.

A guide could describe the opportunities available through digital services, explain how to get the best out the digital age, and publicise national and local services that become available.

There might also be a wider role for education programming. The cross-platform advantage that the BBC currently has over other educational providers could be exploited in a digital age. BBC education expanding the amount of educational materials and software it produces is one way.

If the BBC can develop interactive educational content using digital technology it may widen enormously the understanding of interactivity among the population. This in turn could help break the Internet out of its current niche and into mass usage. Doing so would put the BBC at the cutting edge of this expanding global field.

The digital age presents a challenge for the BBC on all fronts. Its market share will be challenged. It will have to battle for space and viewers attention. Yet if the BBC can be the digital provider of content which is seen to be most interested in securing the benefits of the new age for the whole of society, then it will continue to enjoy a unique position in serving the socially excluded.

Notes

1   After housing costs.

2   All these statistics are cited in *Report of the Commission on Social Justice* (IPPR, 1994).

3   Howarth, C *et al, Key indicators of poverty and social exclusion* by New Policy Institute, 1998.

4   Social Exclusion Unit Website, 1998 (www.open.gov.uk/co/seu).

5   Perri 6 *Escaping Poverty: from safety nets to networks of opportunity* (Demos, 1997).

6   Atkinson, A *Social Exclusion, Poverty and Unemployment* (from *Exclusion, Employment and Opportunity*, Atkinson & Hills [eds], CASE Paper 4, LSE 1998).

7   Seyd & Whiteley conclude that the average Labour Party member is 'a middle-aged, middle-class man' (*Labour's Grass Roots*, Clarendon, 1992) and the average Conservative Party member is 'from a middle-class occupational background' (*True Blues*, Oxford University Press, 1994). This appears to be a growing trend in both organisations.

8   The best indicators of truancy are: living with only one parent, having parents from lower socio-economic groups or who are unemployed, and living in social housing (Pearce and Hillman, *Wasted Youth*, IPPR, 1998)

9   Over half the intake at Oxbridge in 1997 were from Independent schools.

10 An area, often in inner cities, where fresh food is not readily available due to the dependence on convenience stores.

11 Table 1.13, *Report of the Commission on Social Justice* (IPPR, 1994).

12 Page 9, *Our Healthier Nation*, Department of Health, 1998.

13 The work of the IPPR, the Child Poverty Action Group and the Employment Policy Institute have been particularly instructive.

14 Since 1979 the top two-fifths of pensioners have seen their income grow by two-thirds in real terms but the bottom fifth have seen only a 10 per cent increase - *Report of the Commission on Social Justice* (IPPR, 1994).

15 *Lone Parents into Employment*, National Council for One Parent Families, 1997.

16 *Economic Report* (Employment Policy Institute, June 1998).

17 15 per cent of 20-29 yr. old men have been unemployed for more than three years compared to 6 per cent of women – *Office of National Statistics Social trends 28* (TSO, 1998)

18 Pearce & Hillman, *Wasted Youth* (IPPR, 1998).

19 *Employment Audit*, Issue Eight (Employment Policy Institute, Summer 1998).

20 Adonis & Pollard *A Class Act* (Hamish Hamilton, 1997).

21 Initially truancy, homelessness and the worst housing estates; the next priorities will be teenage parents and 16-18 year olds.

22 Hutton, W*The State We're In*, (Vintage, 1996).

23 See the Benton Foundation *Losing Ground Bit by Bit: Low income communities in the information age* (Benton Foundation, 1998) for what has happened in the USA.

24 Higher elderly dependency ratio (DSS Annual Report).

25 For example consumer goods and insurance companies targeting older customers.

26 BBC Annual Report.

27 *The World in Figures* (Economist, 1998).

28 *Office for National Statistics Social Trends 28* (TSO, 1998).

29 *Office for National Statistics Social Trends 28* (TSO, 1998).

30 *The Many Faces of the UK* (BBC Policy & Planning, 1998).

31 Between 1992 and 1998 ITV's share of audience fell 10 per cent from 42 per cent to 32 per cent. During the same period the BBC's share fell 2 per cent from 43 per cent to 41 per cent (BARB).

32 Although the gap has narrowed commercial broadcasters still retain a ten-point lead over the BBC when people are asked 'who pays most attention to public opinion?' (*BBC Corporate Image Study*, Quarter 2, 1998).

33 Frost, M 'One year old but bubbly's on ice', *Broadcast*, 6 November 1998.

34 Adonis & Pollard (*A Class Act*, Hamish Hamilton, 1997) claim that the BBC makes programmes targeted at difference class groups. A less extreme view is that the BBC boxes groups like the disabled and ethnic minorities into special programming.

35 Graham, A *Broadcasting Policy in the Multimedia Age*, this volume.

36 Overall rating of the BBC is 63 per cent positive (*BBC Corporate Image Study*, Quarter 2, 1998).

37 People cite 'trustworthy', 'influential', 'wise' and 'upholding traditional values' among their top BBC attributes (*BBC Corporate Image Study*, Quarter 2, 1998).

38 *BBC News: The Future*, BBC, 1998.

39 The Licence Fee is 4 per cent of the average households weekly leisure spend and 9 per cent for the bottom fifth of households – ONS Social Trends 28 (TSO, 1998).

40 For the average adult the BBC costs 23p an hour – author's calculations.

41 The UK has the fifth lowest Licence Fee in Europe – Prima Europe research.

42 See Congdon, T *et al. Paying for Broadcasting* (Routledge, 1992) for a summary.

43 For example as the government allows more people under 65 year into the homes they become disqualified.

44 *Report of the Committee on Financing the BBC* (HM Stationary Office, 1986).

45 Hotels purchase one licence fee for the first fifteen sets and one per five sets thereafter.

46 Internal BBC figures.

47 *BBC Annual Report 1997/98* (BBC, 1998).

48 Murroni & Irvine (*Access Matters*, IPPR, 1998) quote BBC figures suggesting that 60 per cent of non-payment households earn less than £100 a week.

49 For example 'Computers don't Bite' led 92,000 people to try a computing lesson for the first time.

50 Internal BBC Education report, July 1998.

51 Page 13, Murroni & Irvine *Access Matters* (IPPR, 1998).

52 *Extending Choice in the Digital Age* (BBC, 1996).

53 Murroni & Irvine *Access Matters* (IPPR, 1998).

54 *The BBC Beyond 2000* (BBC, 1998).

55 See Fuller, J *New Values – ideas for an information age* (University of Chicago Press, 1996).

Notes on Contributors

Andrew Graham is Acting Master and Fellow in Economics at Balliol College, Oxford. He recently lead an ESRC research project into public policy aspects of the Information Superhighway and was from 1988 to 1994 Economic Adviser to the Rt Hon John Smith QC, MP. He is a board member of Channel 4 Television.

Christian Koboldt is a Managing Consultant at London Economics, specialising in Media and Telecommunications regulation and policy.

Sarah Hogg is Chairman of London Economics and former Head of the Downing Street Policy Unit. A life peer, she is a member of the House of Lords Science and Technology Committee which investigated barriers to the development of the information society. She is on the board of a number of public companies and research organisations.

Bill Robinson is Director of the Strategy and Policy Practice at London Economics, former Special Adviser to the Chancellor of the Exchequer and former Director of the Institute for Fiscal Studies.

David Currie is Director of the Regulation Initiative and Professor of Economics at the London Business School. In October 1996, he was elevated to the House of Lords as Lord Currie of Marylebone. His current research interests include government regulation of industry and competition policy.

Martin Siner is a Research Officer at the London Business School. He holds degrees in Economics from Kingston University and Birkbeck College.

Graham Mather MEP is Conservative spokesman on economics, monetary and industrial policy in the European Parliament and a member of the shadow Treasury team at Westminster. Since 1996 he has been President of the European Media Forum, a think tank specialising in the convergent broadcast, communications and electronic commerce sectors.

Julian Le Grand is Richard Titmuss Professor of Social Policy at the London School of Economics and a Professional Fellow of the Kings Fund. He is the author, co-author or editor of over sixty articles and seven books on the welfare state. he acts as advisor to the World Bank, the European Commission, the World Health Organisation and various Government departments on social security and health policy.

Bill New is a PhD student at the LSE, developing theories of state intervention in welfare provision. He was also for many years a health policy analyst at the King's Fund with a special interest in issues of rationing and accountability.

Ian Corfield is Business Manager to Sir Dennis Stevenson CBE, Chairman of Pearson Plc. Before this he was Research Director at the Fabian Society and before that a retail strategist with Andersen Consulting. In 1997, he was a member of the panel examining the management of the BBC chaired by Baroness Smith of Gilmorehill. He writes in a personal capacity.

Index